THE PRICE OF AFFLUENCE

THE PRICE OF AFFLUENCE

Dilemmas of Contemporary Japan

Rokurō Hidaka

KODANSHA INTERNATIONAL LTD.
Tokyo, New York and San Francisco

Distributed in the United States by Kodansha International/USA Ltd., through
Harper & Row, Publishers, Inc., 10 East 53rd Street, New York, New York
10022. Published by Kodansha International Ltd., 12-21, Otowa 2-chome,
Bunkyo-ku, Tokyo 112 and Kodansha International/USA Ltd., with offices
at 10 East 53rd Street, New York, New York 10022 and The Hearst Building,
5 Third Street, Suite 430, San Francisco, California 94103.

Originally published under the title *Sengo shisō o kangaeru* by Iwanami Shoten.
Copyright © 1980 by Rokurō Hidaka.
English translation copyright © 1984 by Kodansha International Ltd.
All rights reserved. Printed in Japan.
First English edition, 1984.

Library of Congress Cataloging in Publication Data
Hidaka, Rokurō, 1917–

The price of affluence.

Translation of: Sengo Shisō o kangaeru.
1. Japan—History—1945–   . I. Title.
DS889.H47313   1984   952.04   83-48875
ISBN 0-87011-655-X
ISBN 4-7700-1155-5 (in Japan)

CONTENTS

Preface

Believing in the myth of the divine origins of the country and the invincibility of the Imperial Army, pre-1945 Japan presented an arrogant face to the world, and to Asia in particular. With the defeat in August of 1945, however, the Japanese people realized that they must relearn the universal values of peace, democracy, and fundamental human rights. As a result, they became quite humble.

However, with the rapid growth of the economy from the 1960s onward, which has attracted worldwide attention and led to calls for the emulation of Japan's industrial policy and management practices, the Japanese have become overly confident in the country's economic prowess and once again are falling prey to arrogance. The reemergence of such arrogance, especially among bureaucrats and businessmen, is not, I believe, a good sign for the future. Needless to say, unlike certain Japanese intellectuals, I am not masochistically critical of everything Japanese. Indeed, I feel positive that, for the time being at least, there is little danger that the general public will get caught up in any ultranationalistic madness like that of prewar days. The hatred of war has spread roots in Japan that are quite deep. It is precisely to this fact that I would like to draw the reader's attention.

In 1979 the Soviet Union invaded Afghanistan. While the Soviet people no doubt believed in the justice of their cause, the Japanese people were critical of the action. In 1982 British and Argentinean forces clashed over the Falkland Islands, and support for Mrs. Thatcher, which had been on the decline, suddenly soared. But the Japanese people were unimpressed with what seemed a throwback to nineteenth-century imperialist disputes over territorial rights. In 1983 US forces suddenly invaded Grenada, and President Reagan's waning popularity showed a remarkable recovery. But this action, too, was strongly criticized by a majority of the Japanese people.

All three of these countries were among the victors in the Second World War. War patriotism, and the mass media to fan it, still exist there. In contrast, as a result of being on the losing side, the Japanese people have learned to hate war.

While it is true that war patriotism does not exist in Japan, economic patriotism grows stronger year by year, reaching the level of arrogance. Born and raised in China before the Second World War, I cannot help seeing parallels between this phenomenon and the arrogance of the Japanese people toward Asia before the war. Furthermore, if this economic patriotism were to develop into military patriotism, that would not only spell disaster for Japan but would undoubtedly prove a menace to Japan's neighbors.

There is no denying that Japan's economic growth has, for the present, freed the people from poverty as they used to know it. But it is also a fact that economic prosperity has given birth to a new problem of an extremely serious nature. There is of course the matter of the destruction of our natural environment, but what I would like to draw attention to here is the fact that the exclusive pursuit of profit and efficiency has resulted in the establishment of a controlled society that, while not militaristic, is under extremely tight constraints and, by extension, has led to the formation of a controlled state.

This is the problem that I have attempted to describe in this book. Indeed, the livelihood, culture, education, and leisure of the people is becoming standardized and passive. At a deep level people's minds are held in thrall by the vision of a "comfortable life," which is a product of this age of mass production and mass consumption. This consciousness spurs people to struggle among themselves to secure a position on the path to a good life that has been laid out for them in society and is ready for use. What has emerged is not an authoritarian or totalitarian society, but something I call a controlled society. It is characterized by induced integration rather than oppressive control. But the path that people are induced to follow is surprisingly narrow, and the sense of loss of purpose is spreading, especially among young people, as they are deprived of opportunities for self-expression and self-fulfillment.

This phenomenon is not confined to Japan, but seems rather to be common to all highly industrialized countries. In fact, it might be called a malaise of the times. While suffering from the same sickness, however, each country exhibits peculiar symptoms according to its history and traditions. I hope that this book will help, however slightly, toward an understanding of the condition in contemporary Japan.

I am indebted to many people for help in bringing this book to publication and would like to express my deep gratitude to them.

First, I owe a debt to Professors Sugimoto and Gavan McCormack of La Trobe University, who have played a major role in promoting this English edition. In particular, Professor McCormack put a great deal of effort into the editing and coordinating of the original translated manuscript. The task of translation was divided among various Japan scholars in Australia, whose names are noted elsewhere, and I am of course grateful to all of them.

In Japan, I am thankful for the help of my university colleagues, especially Nakao Hajime, and also Mr. Nobuki Saburō, managing-director of Kodansha International and a former student of mine at Tokyo University, who was enthusiastic about the publication of an English-language edition. To Ichiba Shinji and Michael Brase, on the staff of Kodansha International, and to editor Paul Waley, I am most grateful.

There are many more to whom I feel grateful, numbering in the hundreds. The two-and-a-half-year period between 1981 and 1983 was a time of great personal difficulty. Many friends were kind enough to come to my aid. To these friends, both in Japan and Australia, I offer my deepest thanks.

Let me briefly explain here the situation that I refer to. In January 1981, at the invitation of La Trobe and Monash Universities in Melbourne, Australia, I had planned to spend approximately ten months in Australia engaged in teaching and research. The Japan Foundation, an organization affiliated to the Japanese government, had promised full financial backing. However, on the eve of departure, the Australian government refused visas to me and my wife for security reasons. Without going into detail, suffice it to say that I protested strongly against this completely baseless decision. At the same time, hundreds of friends in Japan signed appeals asking that the Australian government reconsider the matter. Among the signers were some of Japan's most respected intellectuals, professors, and diplomats. One Australian newspaper reported that the list read like a Japanese who's who. In Australia, the effort devoted by university people and intellectuals to this problem was greater than I could ever have imagined. The fact that neither of the two universities cancelled my invitation is admirable in itself. Eventually, in July of 1983, the misunderstanding that my wife and I were connected with a "violent terrorist" organization, a notion pronounced laughable by those who heard it, was resolved, much to the credit of the Australian government. In September of that year, the universities renewed the invitation and I was able to pay a short visit and deliver four public lectures.

I shall never forget the friendship and encouragement shown me by my friends in Australia and Japan during the so-called

Hidaka affair. The publication of this book is due in large part to friends in Australia seeing some merit in it, but it was also prompted in part by this affair. At this time, friendship crossed national boundaries. Now my book, too, has crossed national boundaries.

Hidaka Rokurō
Paris
22 April 1984

Note on the Translation

The Japanese text of this book was published in Tokyo by Iwanami Shoten in December 1980 under the title *Sengo shisō o kangaeru.*
Initial draft English translations were prepared by the following:

Ch. 1. Ross Mouer, Griffith University, Brisbane.

Ch. 2, Concluding Remarks, Appendix. Gavan McCormack, La Trobe University, Melbourne.

Ch. 3. Jiri Neustupny, Monash University, Melbourne.

Ch. 4. Yoshio Sugimoto, La Trobe University, Melbourne.

Ch. 5. Peter Davidson, Margaret Price, and Evaline Rawlinson, University of Queensland, Brisbane.

Ch. 6. Elizabeth Mouer, Armidale College of Advanced Education, Armidale.

Ch. 7. Nanette Twine, Griffith University, Brisbane.

Ch. 8. John and Katsu Young and Peter Chapman, West Australian Institute of Technology, Perth.

Coordination, revision, and editing of the final English text was done by Gavan McCormack, with the assistance of Yoshio Sugimoto.

Gavan McCormack
(Editor and Translator-in-chief)
La Trobe University, Melbourne

▌▌▌ Chapter One ▌▌▌

Reflections on Thought
in the Postwar Period

I

I lecture on the history of postwar thought at a college in Kyoto. But so often the semester passes without us getting beyond talk of the wartime period. Eventually I come to discuss Miki Kiyoshi's* death in prison and its significance. The students, mostly young women, are fresh from high school, but they appear quite interested, and they come to my weekly lecture. Sitting below my lecture platform, they look resplendent in their bright, colorful clothes. They listen with great interest as I discuss the events surrounding Miki's death. Without a doubt, this is the first time that most of them have heard his name.

As I look over the sea of bright, eager faces, I suddenly realize that none of the students is aged over twenty; to them I am already an old man.

There are students who come up to me and tell me how fascinating it is to hear about all these events of which they knew nothing. It is like listening to the history of centuries past,

---

*Prominent philosopher (1897–1945). Imprisoned in 1930 for opposition to the Public Peace Preservation Law, he later cooperated with the wartime administration's propaganda department (in 1942), but was again arrested in 1944 for harboring a Communist sympathizer. He died in prison in September 1945, more than a month after the end of the war.—Trans.

they say. So I try to avoid referring to the present constitution as the "new constitution." Rather, I simply refer to it as the "Japanese constitution" or the "present constitution." Above all, I hope the students will not take what I say as a tale out of the dim, distant past.

At the same time, it is not I but these young women who are most vividly experiencing the present. Although I may know a good deal more than them about the structure of politics, society, and the economy in contemporary Japan, they are much more sensitive to the portentous and murky atmosphere that now envelops the country. Though I am not Goethe's Faust it may be that I possess a certain "gray theory" to leave as my legacy. These students confront me as so many fresh green sprouts of life itself.

I tell the students that Miki Kiyoshi did not die before 15 August 1945, when the war ended, but that he died in prison on 26 September, over a month later. I then relate something I heard from Nakajima Kenzō. Miki apparently died from malnutrition and sleeplessness after having contracted scabies. It is suspected that he contracted scabies because he was given the blankets of another prisoner who was suffering from the same disease. In other words, he would seem to have been the victim of a cleverly contrived murder. On the morning of 26 September, a guard opened the door of Miki's cell and found his body on the floor. He had somehow fallen off his hard wooden bed onto the floor and died there, shriveled up like a piece of dried fish.

Even after the end of the war, the government failed to release Miki. Nor was anyone able to help him. As a result, Japan lost a thinker who might have made a great intellectual contribution to the postwar world.

And when I go on to say that Miki's death in prison led to the fall of the cabinet of Prince Higashikuni, and to state that the anger of a single person over the denial of human rights to another person toppled the government, the students sit in rapt attention. Needless to say, most of the students know nothing of these events.

It was a foreign correspondent with Reuter who, on hearing the news of Miki's death in prison, investigated the circumstances. He learned that political prisoners were all still in prison. The astonished correspondent sought an interview with the home affairs minister, Yamazaki Iwao, who told him, "The secret police in charge of thought control are still active. They will without hesitation arrest communists who carry out propaganda against the imperial house. . . . We will continue to detain communist party members. All persons advocating change in the form of government, especially abandonment of the imperial system, will be regarded as communists and arrested under the Public Peace Preservation Law." The interview was published on 4 October in the *Stars and Stripes* (the newspaper for officers and personnel of the US armed forces). It immediately caused a stir, and that evening General MacArthur ordered "the release of political prisoners and the removal of all restrictions on the freedoms associated with political, religious, and human rights." The cabinet of Prince Higashikuni was at a loss, and resigned. On 9 October the Shidehara cabinet was formed. On 10 October all political prisoners were released, among their number being some who had spent eighteen years in prison.

It is farcical that for two and a half months after surrender, the minister of home affairs went nonchalantly about his business, believing he enjoyed the support of MacArthur's headquarters, and giving voice to his convictions in this way. As a result of this outrage, the tragic death of Miki Kiyoshi occurred.

The nature of the surrender was revealed in the fact that no one clamored for the release of political prisoners or even gathered at the prisons and detention centers to inquire about Miki and other political prisoners on the day the war ended. Nor was there any protest in the few days or even during the months that followed. I urge my students to confirm this with their own eyes by thumbing page by page through the newspapers published in the period following the end of the war. I want them to know that the historical account according to which militarism collapsed all of a sudden on 15 August and gave way to the age of democracy is actually far from the truth. The process of change was gradual, like a slow-motion film.

With the defeat of Germany and Italy and the fall of the Vichy government in France, change in those countries was immediate and clear-cut. The past was condemned at once. Political prisoners were released without delay; war criminals were quickly rounded up. In Japan, however, both the leadership and the press strove to sustain the dying militarism. It was as though they were struggling to save a desperately ill patient by first administering thin rice soup, then rice gruel, and finally rice itself. First, it was said that democracy meant unity of the sovereign and his people, and then that the Five Article Charter Oath* was democracy, that the Constitution of the Great Japanese Empire was based on the spirit of democracy, and that the principles of parliamentary government had existed since Meiji times (1868–1912). In due course, it was said that only parliamentary democracy in the Anglo-American tradition was to be acknowledged as true democracy. The newspapers that had cooperated with the wartime policy continued on into the postwar period through all these gradual changes and cleverly exploited them. They did not even change their names. No such thing happened with German, Italian, or Vichy French newspapers.

I tell the students that it was not a Japanese reporter but a foreign correspondent who learned of Miki's death and approached the minister of home affairs. On the part of the foreign correspondent, at least, there was some concern for human rights. After expressing his surprise and indignation to the minister, he visited MacArthur's headquarters to lodge a complaint there. MacArthur's officials were obliged to accept the legitimacy of his argument.

---

*A statement issued in March 1868 by the Meiji emperor in the form of an oath to his imperial ancestors. It was adopted later as a basic policy document of the new Meiji government.—Trans.

These events also make it clear that it was not only the Japanese masses who failed to demand the release of prisoners after the end of the war. The Japanese government, MacArthur's headquarters, and the Allied Council for Japan also failed to do so. Rather, the matter was raised by a foreign journalist who was a private citizen. It is with these events in mind that I say the anger of one human being over the violation of the human rights of another caused the downfall of the Higashikuni cabinet.

II

Next, I go on to speak about the International Military Tribunal for the Far East.

On 23 December 1948 the nation's newspapers published the following news. Large headlines in the *Asahi* read, "Execution by hanging of seven war criminals, including Tōjō,* carried out at 00.25 A.M. this morning." Below this was an article headed "Covered truck travels Keihin National Highway— seven coffins aboard?" One can also read in the inside pages of the same day's paper the heading, "With prayer beads clasped in his hand, Tōjō speeds toward Paradise; condemned men circulate a copy of *Shinran*† among themselves."

I then proceed to direct the students' attention to a tiny item on the same page. The heading is "First indictments against the 'Coal Officials': Tanaka, Kiso, and Haraguchi." The reference is to the story of how coal mine owners in north Kyushu who opposed national control of the coal mines had paid a bribe of one million yen to Tanaka Kakuei, dietman for the then Democratic Liberal Party, former parliamentary vice-minister of justice, and future prime minister. Both sides were indicted.

---

*1884–1948. General and prime minister of Japan from 1941 to 1944; executed in 1948 as a war criminal.—Trans.

†Shinran (1173–1262). Buddhist monk who founded the Pure Land sect of Japanese Buddhism.—Trans.

This is another episode in postwar history. Leaving it aside for the moment, however, I pick up the paper for two days later, 25 December. The headlines read: "19 class-A indictees, including Kishi, released; processing of major war criminals brought to a close." I leave out detailed explanations about each of the nineteen. However, the students' interest is aroused by three names they know well: Kishi Nobusuke (minister of commerce and industry during the war, and future prime minister), Kodama Yoshio (founder of the Kodama Organ in Shanghai), and Sasagawa Ryōichi (president of the National Essence Mass Party [Kokusui Taishūtō] during the war). But I also draw attention to one other name: Abe Genki (minister of home affairs during the war and a member of the Diet after it). He had long been connected with the thought-control police (*tokkō keisatsu*), and I want the students to know what sort of role the *tokkō* played.

I like to recall as accurately as possible and to discuss with the students the complex feelings of somber elation I had on that cold winter's morning when I heard the news of the execution of the class-A war criminals. What was the makeup of those complex emotions? Two days later came news of the release of the nineteen war-crime suspects. For one lot, the gallows; for the other, acquittal and release. Although right and wrong may seem to be like light and dark, when one thinks of the wartime deeds of the acquitted, the injustice is obvious to anyone. I was deeply shocked when I heard this news; I experienced a sense of dread, as though the eyes of the *tokkō* secret police were once again haunting my surroundings. For I did not understand very well why this should have happened or why it was significant.

As the Cold War intensified, however, I came to understand its significance very clearly. Kodama, Sasagawa, and Kishi were released because they had to be released. Their release was in line with the logical thrust of American world strategy. The execution of Tōjō and the other war criminals was simply a symbolic ritual to put the war behind us. Was postwar history altered by the execution of Tōjō and the others? It did have a certain effect. But what about the release of Kishi and company? I believe this had a greater subsequent influence. Upon reflection, it may be that it was the release of the nineteen rather than the execution of the Tōjō group which was the greater historical event. On the one hand, there is deception and opportunism in America's policy toward Japan. On the other hand, there is the weakness of the Japanese people and, even if for obvious reasons, of the Japanese government, which was unable to solve the problem of war crimes by itself.

I turn next to the year 1976 and the Lockheed affair,* in which Kodama Yoshio, who was released on 24 December 1948, emerges as the central figure. In the scandal of the Lockheed-Grumman aircraft, former Prime Minister Kishi enters the picture. The students can probably piece these facts together themselves.

It is at this point that the students begin to ask questions. "What do adults in postwar Japan think about their failure to help Miki Kiyoshi or to deal with their own war criminals?" Standing at the lectern, I am always aware that a certain number of students harbor such doubts. Why is it that those who talk about responsibility for the war avoid responsibility for what happened after the war? After the defeat, young people often questioned their elders:

"Did none of you consider the unjustness of the Sino-Japanese War or the recklessness of the Pacific War?"

"Yes, many of us did. Around the time of the Manchurian Incident there were journals like *Kaizō* and *Chūō kōron.* . . ."

"Then why didn't you protest?"

"Protest? But there were dreadful laws like the Public Peace Preservation Law in force at the time."

---

*One of a series of corruption scandals which shook Japan in the 1970s, involving the payment of huge bribes by Lockheed Corporation to prominent Japanese politicians and officials in an attempt to secure lucrative contracts.— Trans.

From the look on the faces of the young of those days, it was clear they were unsure how far they could believe these answers. When the young of today ask the same sort of questions about the postwar situation, how are we, the adult generation, to reply?

"Why is it that the progressive forces of the postwar period have been unable to usurp power from the likes of Kodama, war criminals who have survived through all these long years?"

When questioned in this manner by my students, how should I reply? "Well, there were various weaknesses. We were unable to make a clean sweep of the old prewar faces. There were changes in the international situation. Besides, the democratic forces misread the situation, and we were unable to put down roots among the people."

A reply of this kind is unlikely to satisfy the young. This is why I must lecture on the history of thought in the postwar period.

III

Miki's death in prison, the execution of Tōjō and the six other class-A war criminals, and then the acquittal and release of Kodama, Kishi, and the others: these matters of life and death teach us a good deal. It is as if the postwar period were illuminated in this one set of events. This seems all the more so if one considers how those who were given a new lease on life later became central figures in the Lockheed affair.

The inability of the Japanese to rescue Miki Kiyoshi from prison or to tackle by themselves the problem of bringing war criminals to justice is directly connected to the fact that a movement capable of putting an end to the war did not develop among the Japanese people (although there were secret moves involving a group of prominent people of liberal disposition). Unfortunately, popular strength was lacking. Plenty of people were conscious enough of the facts to criticize the war. Some were thrown into prison for doing so. But they did not constitute a force capable of changing the course of history.

Herein lies a lesson. But have we reached the point even now of being able to overcome this powerlessness of ours?

In connection with the death of Miki Kiyoshi, I speak also to my students of the Japanese government's astonishing sensitivity to order and its total lack of concern for human rights. I also point out the lack of interest in the fate of political criminals on the part of MacArthur's staff. And I draw attention to the greatness of the active efforts of a single private journalist.

In 1976, Donald Ranard (former director of the Office of Korean Affairs in the US Department of State) testified to an American congressional committee that the Korean Central Intelligence Agency had been responsible for the abduction of Kim Dae Jung from Japan. However, when the opposition parties raised the issue in the Japanese Diet, the government spokesman said the matter could not be pursued further since Ranard had retired from public service and was now a private citizen. I find the combination of delicate sensitivity toward bureaucratic self-protection and insensitivity toward human rights astonishing. Even MacArthur's headquarters, which issued an order for the release of political prisoners when faced with the complaint of a journalist, was better than this, however unpalatable it may be to admit it.

The Lockheed affair and the various other cases of corruption which have come to light since then are very revealing. Their structure, their background, and the manner in which they unfolded are all important. There is, however, another important element. That is the problem of how organizations and people react to the incidents. This has to be considered alongside the question of corruption itself. Government, political parties, business, media, and the public: what stand does each of these segments of society take? What does each try to do? Some of those who gave or received money will be—in some cases, have already been—punished by the courts. But this will be like the ritual of executing the Tōjō group. Just as Kodama, Sasagawa, and others were released from Sugamo Prison and restored to life, so now most of the suspects in these cases will recover. But will this really resolve the problem of corruption? How can endemic corruption be thoroughly eliminated? What methods are necessary? Would it be possible to implement such methods in today's Japan? Is anyone seriously discussing such questions or proposing solutions? In the ranks of the government and the majority party I think it is safe to say that there is no one. To me, *this* is the basis from which the cases of corruption have sprung.

One problem emerges from the continued corruption: is it possible for there to be a Liberal Democratic Party (LDP) which is not corrupt? Can there really be clean Japanese capitalism? These are major questions for conservative business leaders and politicians. In my view, it is difficult to compartmentalize—to think of the LDP as consisting of three groups: the good, the bad, and the in-between. It is also difficult for capitalism to exist without corruption. But conservative leaders in the political and business world would certainly not accept this view. In their opinion, at least the LDP can be cleaned up and capitalism made socially conscious. If they think that way, however, why don't they draw lessons from the many incidents of corruption and launch earnest discussion on how best to clean out their own house? In particular, what are we to make of the attitude of indifference shown by people in business? This indifference strikes me as nothing less than irresponsibility.

If political and business leaders are indeed convinced that talk of clean government and clean capitalism is only for public consumption, while actually believing that such things are not realistic, and if they support the present system on the basis of such convictions, the result is nihilism. I do not wish to be ruled by nihilists. Nihilist thinking presumably goes like this: capitalism can exist only if it is corrupt, but since some people must be ruled by others, the only alternative is to use force and guile. However such thinking may be rationalized, it is authoritarianism.

At the time of the Watergate affair in the United States, many political and financial leaders criticized President Nixon. They sought to defend the liberal system. They believed that the liberal system possessed the capacity to recover, and they were prepared to join together in their commitment to this belief. But if it is true to say that "he who speaks out will suffer for it," that "the protruding nail will be beaten down," and that "to do business one must be prepared to kowtow," then force alone rules, and idealistic elements are completely lacking. What, therefore, does the "liberal" ingredient in the expression "liberal economy" mean to Japanese politicians and businessmen? Does it mean no more than the freedom to buy and to sell and to make a profit? Do they seriously believe that there is no need to worry about the future of a "free" market economy sustained by such unprincipled liberalism?

This same tendency is evident in the position taken by the Japanese mass media. After the war those who ran the wartime press argued, in effect, that the newspapers were large enterprises responsible for the well-being of a great number of employees, a fact which gave them no alternative but to cooperate with the policies of the government of the time. By keeping their opinions to themselves they protected their employees from being thrown out onto the streets; but in the process they became mere benevolent societies, not organs of opinion. It would have been more honest of them to have admitted they were not prepared to put the fate of their enterprise on the line. The postwar media were born out of reflections on these facts. At least, they should have been. However, in Japan a subtle change of direction occurred shortly after the war. The initiative taken by the press in the Watergate affair and the activities of the *New York Times* or the *Washington Post*, which published the "Pentagon Papers," is not to be found in the

Japanese press. American newspapers pursued their criticisms and set out clearly their objectives before the announcement from the prosecutors. They relentlessly pursued an incumbent president. One could not expect the mass media in Japan to play such an active role.

A serious passivity (in other words, irresponsibility) pervades political and economic circles and the media in Japan. Some politicians and businessmen probably hoped for a thorough cleanup after the corruption scandals had broken. But they did not take the initiative, and the conduct of the operation passed to others. No one called out for a clear allocation of responsibility. It may be possible to bring someone else in to perform an operation and administer therapy in the case of a physical ailment, but clearly not in the case of moral degeneration.

The fact that many of the corruption scandals have been brought to light via sources in the United States is more than symbolic. In the United States, it is recognized that if the liberal system becomes too corrupt, it is weakened overall. I am inclined to think that the time will come when, either from the American side or under a new Korean regime, the corruption of the Japan–South Korea connection will be exposed. But it will not be exposed *from within Japan*. Has anything at all changed in the pattern of Japan since the surrender of 15 August 1945?

IV

Unprincipled support for a liberal economic system in effect means support for a policy of profits first without any notion of fair play. The deep-rooted opposition of business to any tightening-up of the antimonopoly legislation underlines this fact.

Nevertheless, it is through economic success that postwar Japan has made such great advances. The achievement is a startling one. After overtaking Britain and West Germany and becoming the free world's second greatest economic power, Japanese business has become very self-confident. To what extent has this success caused the destruction of nature and the environment in Japan? To what extent is it causing resentment among the politicians and business leaders and especially the ordinary people in the developing countries of the Third World? I leave this question for another time.

The business world in Japan will be very hard to budge. Their thinking probably goes something like this: "If conservative government fails, we can try a coalition government; if that fails, we can try a reformist government; and if that fails, there is always fascism." What is it that sustains this confidence? Certainly one major factor has been the increase in the standard of living during the postwar period. But what does the improvement in living standards really mean? Has the quality of life improved? How much of the population is included in the strata whose living standards have improved?

Although many of us are skeptical about the consequences, it is difficult to deny that life has become much more comfortable for most. Indeed, many are becoming imprisoned by their sense of comfort.

Just as support for a free economic system without moral principles becomes an ideology justifying the unhindered pursuit of profit, so support for a democratic system in which the sense of the people as rulers is abandoned becomes a materialistically oriented ideology justifying only an increase in creature comforts and the material standard of living. Business has striven to provide a section of the people with democracy, but it has been a democracy "by and for business" not "by and for the people." And, to a certain extent, it has succeeded.

Both ruling and opposition parties are united in their pursuit of improved living standards and increased comfort. When presented in these terms, it is hard to disagree. And yet, to be quite honest, I see a serious problem arising out of the political consensus on this point. I think the time is coming when we will have to seriously reconsider the idea of simply "improving the standard of living," not to mention the notion of "increased comfort."

I trust no one will jump to the conclusion that my opinion

resembles the philosophy propounded by the business elite. The French intellectual Georges Friedman proposed that objects of need be sharply distinguished from objects of desire. Human beings must decide with care the objects that are really necessary to life. A man who is driven by the dictates of greed actually diminishes his happiness in life and his sense of liberty. To be sovereign in the political world, man must also be master in the sphere of his daily life. This constitutes the first problem for the philosophy of comfort. Now we worship the consumer as king but at the same time consign him to slavery, the slavery of the advertisement and of the market place. A philosophy which would dissent from this process must take a stand that is flatly opposed to the philosophy of business.

Of course, I know that there are deprived places in Japan, where many people on a low income have no guaranteed livelihood let alone the prospect of increased comfort. For those who exist in this way, an improvement in living standards is truly an "object of necessity." Furthermore, I am also aware of the insufficiency of social capital. Here too we have an "object of necessity." The difficult job of distinguishing between "objects of necessity" and "objects of desire" cannot simply be reduced to the issue of the quantity of wealth versus its quality. It has also to do with attitudes to life and toward the spiritual and psychological realm. The question arises as to whether the individual faced today with capital's endless enticements to consume and to enjoy can be free to work out his own way of life.

Visit any wedding hall nowadays and you will find signs proclaiming the wedding ceremony of family X and family Y. In the years immediately after Japan's defeat in the war, many Japanese felt an aversion to the idea that marriages were between families. The ceremonies were simpler then. Today, however, even the labor union member who supports the progressive political parties thinks nothing of going through all the elaborate rituals of the conventional wedding. In some of the rural areas it has become common practice to shower the bride with all the latest household electrical appliances and a lavish wardrobe costing millions of yen. This behavior cannot be understood simply in terms of the rising standard of living. It constitutes a ritual incorporation of the individual into the society ruled by these conventions. It is a ritual of passage by which one allows oneself to be controlled.

The second problem is that the ''increased comfort'' which is either being positively sought by the people or provided for them regardless of whether they want it is in fact tied to the increase in pollution at home and to Japanese economic expansion overseas. As Sōhyō (the General Council of Trade Unions of Japan) noted in its policy statement for 1976:

> The continuing advance of Japanese capital into the Southeast Asian region is giving rise to a number of problems. Bearing in mind that labor unions in this region have not yet developed into a powerful force, we must pay particular attention to strengthening our friendship and solidarity with the labor unions of Southeast Asia.

The word ''advance'' was substituted in the final statement for the word ''invasion,'' but there is something more significant about this statement. Even though the union recognized that ''various problems'' have been created in Southeast Asia, they found it difficult to decide on any concrete action. The only people who have directly confronted Japanese corporations and have opposed the export of their pollution are the small citizens' movements, isolated and inadequately supported. Nevertheless, even with their meager strength, they were able to make an impact on some of the chemical firms who sought to relocate their factories in South Korea. Neither the progressive political parties nor the labor unions have participated in this kind of movement. Indeed, more likely they have secretly resented it. The ''improved living standards'' and ''increased comfort'' of many

Japanese workers have depended on the overseas activities of the corporations.

For this reason, conservatives and reformists in Japan are difficult to tell apart, like so many will-o'-the-wisps. And in terms of their philosophy of comfort, the opinions of both are the same.

I believe it is of no mean significance that the Japanese people since the war have grown accustomed to the little bit of comfort they have tasted. Once comfort has been experienced, it is not easily renounced. I too have experienced a measure of comfort. I do not want to launch into hypocritical self-reproach by lamenting the inconsistency of my own words and deeds. There are few who are free from this mild contradiction. Although in themselves trifling, together the small contradictions add up to constitute a formidable social force. The philosophy of comfort has not been just a philosophy. The fact is that the people have been paid in kind by Japanese business. Both the labor unions and the progressive political parties have gone along without protesting.

V

Year by year the number of university students with their own cars increases. Most students lead a modest life, but the number of students who are either very well-off or quite well-off is increasing. This is a tendency, surely, that adults over fifty— including the directors of large enterprises—find disturbing. They would condemn the youths' financial dependence on adults, but among students there appears to be almost no moral criticism or opposition. Many students secretly nurture the wish to have their own car, the only problem being that they do not have the money. It is, for example, already commonplace for middle class families in the United States to have several cars, one each for husband, wife, and children. The only problem is the money needed to buy and maintain a car.

Successful men of fifty and over raise their eyebrows; they

spent their youth during the war or early postwar years, and no doubt they bear the deep imprint of those times of scarcity. Or it may be that they are attached to notions of status and feel that while it is only right they should be chauffeured to and from work, a car is a luxury inappropriate to the status of ordinary company workers or students. But it is a contradiction for the politicians and businessmen who have made Japan what it is today to raise their eyebrows over students having their own cars, since it is they themselves who have produced the high economic growth which has made this possible.

There is something touchingly foolish about the directors of large firms who are pressed by their own sons to buy them cars. The automobile industry is now the core of Japan's manufacturing industry. And it is these men and their colleagues who have developed the subtle stratagems designed to induce people to rush out to buy a car. The Japanese advertising industry, which closely rivals that of the United States in its sophistication, has whipped up this Japanese passion to consume till it is so thick it is almost palpable. No wonder the younger generation are swept off their feet. It has been a case of "aim at the young." It would have been cause for concern for Japanese business if youth had *not* been swayed.

The management of firms manufacturing 750-cc motorcycles know that there is a relationship between the level of sales and the general level of frustration among youth. They will be satisfied with a rising curve in sales while praying that their own sons do not join a motorcycle gang. It is like the editor of a shoddy weekly magazine who puts out each issue hoping his own children do not read what he has published. Young people who exasperate their parents by demanding to have their own car or motorcycle are in fact getting revenge on the adult world. That they should make such demands of adults is surely to be expected. "Why all the fuss?" is the sort of riposte they might well make to their parents.

I often wonder about the wasteland that exists in the minds

of business executives. In their fifties or sixties now, some must have experienced great deprivation and come close to starvation at the end of the war and immediately afterward. As students in the unsettled times following defeat in the war, they would have been enthusiastic readers of Marx. Some would have participated in the student movement. And they would have been among the critics of Japanese militarism and the industrial-financial conglomerates. They too must have had their youthful dream of a new Japan.

To make a living, however, they had to become salaried employees. In due course they realized they had a certain talent; they worked hard to develop it, were recognized by their superiors, and were promoted. How could they have defected along the way? While crossing dangerous bridges, or being urged across, they carved out their present positions. For every one of those in the top echelons of All Nippon Airways and Marubeni who were arrested in the Lockheed affair, there can be no doubt that there were another thousand or even ten thousand guilty of the same offenses who escaped notice. This, then, is "structural corruption": it was not that just the exceptional one in ten thousand was connected with the bribery case, but rather that, for each ten thousand involved, only one was exposed.

I do not wish to suggest that their condition is beyond reprieve. I wonder, however, whether the Japan which they have striven night and day to create is actually the Japan they had dreamed of after the war. I tend to feel there are some, even among the successful, who look back and think that it is not. I read an article by one such man lamenting the way the mountains he had climbed in his student days on his own two feet had now been despoiled by tourist highways.

Their bewilderment is on the one hand a luxury, and on the other, a source of amusement. At the risk of repeating myself, the present Japanese economic system, which guarantees the position of the elite, could not exist if there were no urge on the part of the people to consume. What laments there are, as far as I can see, are but a passing whim. There do not seem to be many among the conservative business elite who have carefully thought this problem through. It is exactly the same psychological structure as that which dictates that the corruption scandals will produce no serious thinking about the state of big business in Japan.

VI

I wonder whether Japan today is not slowly heading in the direction of another 15 August. In the face of what may seem like a rash of corruption scandals, there has been no sign that the conservative business and political leadership is reexamining its own ways. Although some may deplore it when their own children become involved, none of the leaders has shown any inclination to question seriously the philosophy of comfort, which advances day by day and which was constructed by capital. In short, the forces of liberalism in Japan are in the process of losing their moral vitality and their will to engage in a minimal amount of reflection.

At the same time, it can be argued that the progressive forces in Japan are also discarding their own principles. Not that I wish to suggest that we must choose now between capitalism and socialism. But we are losing our sense of immediate outrage over social inequality, averting our eyes from unorganized workers who work in far worse conditions than unionized labor, and we are failing to consider and judge the philosophy of comfort for one segment of the work force, though it is spreading day by day. Yet this is the psychological foundation which allows scandals like the Lockheed affair to occur.

For this reason the crisis we face is not simply a political crisis or economic uncertainty; even less is it a revolutionary crisis. It is the crisis of the continuing gradual self-destruction of both conservative and reformist forces as autonomous entities. The most thoroughly disturbing aspect of this passage toward comprehensive self-destruction rests in the way conservatives and reformists stroll heedless, hand in hand, along the road to ruin. It was like this once before, from the time of the Sino-Japanese War until the beginning of the Pacific War. After 15 August too, was it not similar? We walked or were led up the gentle incline from militarism to democracy. Who could foresee that the transition from militarism to democracy would be so easy? Now, perhaps, we are descending a gentle slope, moving from democracy toward some new kind of managed totalitarianism. The descent is easy, undertaken at an imperceptible speed.

The methods employed by the Japanese military leadership have been described as a "system of irresponsibility." That was the wartime system of irresponsibility. Nowadays a new system of irresponsibility is emerging amid the philosophy of comfort and in the age of peace. I suggested above that I possessed a "gray theory" and that my young students were "fresh green sprouts of life itself." Actually, I have reached an age when the attractions of a life of comfort do not hold much sway with me. Therefore I realize that I am not in a strong position to criticize a society which is flowing in the direction of comfort. It is the "fresh green sprouts of life" of today—those now experiencing the tremendous pull of this attraction—who must overcome this problem. Even while experiencing that pull, it is only when they realize that such comforts are not linked to their ability to enjoy a spontaneous and independent life that they will really become able to overcome the problem created by this attraction.

In the classroom I talk about the history of postwar thought in Japan, but I never get very far. I do not discuss immediate political issues with students. I believe that a major characteristic of contemporary society is revealed in the fact that the totality of our apparently unpolitical everyday life has actually come to assume highly political functions, and so I talk with these mostly apolitical students about how dull it is to spend life as a mechanical doll. This is because I think the heart of the problem for us now is the remolding of our everyday life and consciousness.

‖‖■ Chapter Two ■‖‖

Communicating Personal Experience

I

I was twenty-eight years of age when the war came to an end. I was already an adult, with my own awareness and judgment of myself and my own awareness and judgment of history. Not only that, I was a human being who had tried to exert some influence on his times. The postwar period coincided precisely with the prime of my life.

Thus I speak of *my* history and the history of *my* times to students who are completely lacking in *my* experience. Can they possibly understand what I have to say? That is the first problem. And does it mean anything? That is the second problem.

If I were to speak about the Meiji Restoration of 1868 or about the formation of the ancient state of Japan there might be differences between speaker and listeners in terms of knowledge of the subject, but in a certain sense we would both be equal. This is because neither of us would have had any direct experience of those times. However, the situation becomes very different when I turn to the wartime and postwar periods, for then it is a case not only of degrees of knowledge or of the existence of knowledge but of one who has experience speaking to others who have not.

There is a positive aspect when one with experience speaks to others without. If experience can be translated into knowledge and thought, it becomes possible to imbibe the particular feelings and spirit of the one who had that experience. Particular feelings mean feelings about, first, the overall mood that governs a certain age and, secondly, the detailed events, sometimes important, sometimes mundane, that occurred in that period and were experienced by someone who was alive at the time. The possession of a sense both of the totality and of the detail is the privilege of someone with experience. Yet this ''privilege'' can also make it difficult for the person with experience to communicate with those without experience.

When I talk about the Meiji Restoration, I have no alternative but to do my own research and form my own judgment, using the broadest possible range of literary and historical documents. These documents exist in an objective sense. It is just that the young do not know of them. Both for me and for the young, they have an external existence. From them, we select events and interpretations that are meaningful and reflect on the relationships between them. It can easily happen that we all select the same subjects as meaningful and consider them in a context common to us all. When I am face-to-face with my students in the classroom I am keenly aware of this, and I begin by speaking frankly about these events.

II

When I talk about the years during and after the war I notice three things about the reactions my comments provoke among the students.

First of all, the students are moved by things that I have felt strongly about or been moved by. Secondly, they come to appreciate the connection between the meanings of various events. To some extent students have learned about post-Meiji history or contemporary history up to the Shōwa period in their study of Japanese and world history at high school. But this cannot be taken at face value. Questions about the history of the Shō-wa period scarcely ever appear in university entrance examinations. So there are many junior-high and high-school students who speak either of not having studied anything subsequent to the "Manchurian Incident" of 1931 or of just having been told by their teachers to read up on the rest in their textbooks. In preparation for their various school tests and entrance examinations, they have simply memorized the years in which wars occurred, where they occurred, the name of prime ministers at such times, and the results of the wars. As for the "causes" of the wars, all they remember are meaningless fragments such as that the cause of the Sino-Japanese War was the *fact* that the armies of Japan and China clashed on Marco Polo Bridge in the suburbs of Peking in 1937. It should go without saying that when considering the causes of the confrontations between Japan and China, including the Manchurian Incident, one must go back to the period of international imperialism of the nineteenth century, or, in the case of Japan, to the point when the direction of Japan's post–Meiji-Restoration policy toward Asia was determined. The work of unraveling this thread is almost completely neglected in high-school history education. Education in history at school consists of being made to learn by rote times, places, people, and incidents. When I say that such knowledge does not mean one knows anything about history, and begin to talk about the meaning and relatedness of events, the curiosity of the young begins to stir.

Thirdly, their interest is aroused when I discuss the points of contact between military and political developments on a global scale and the behavior and the everyday life of normal people—farmers, workers, housewives, and students. Their interest is aroused both when I speak of how people spent their days during the war, as if the war had nothing to do with them, and when I show how the greater circumstance of war penetrated their everyday life. It is also aroused when I speak of it being precisely everyday life that sustains and creates the greater circumstance.

III

I once read in the "Koe" (Voice) column in the *Asahi* newspaper a letter written by a woman who had just returned from Indonesia. The gist of the letter was as follows: There are many Japanese families in Indonesia who employ Indonesian helpers. However, the Indonesians are thought by these Japanese to be liars and dirty. And, since people say it would be wrong to appear kind to them, there are some Japanese who will not even return the morning greetings of their Indonesian employees. The woman who wrote this letter made the point that when one thinks of the need for future long-term friendship between Japan and Indonesia this sort of attitude must be criticized.

Before and during the war I was in Qingdao in China. It was the everyday life of the Japanese at that time that immediately came to mind when I read this. In those days there was Chinese domestic help working in almost all Japanese homes in China. A Chinese man was called "boy" and a woman "amah." In the homes of people like senior employees of trading companies, there used to be three or four such employees, including boy, amah, and driver. Where now in Japan would you find a family of four with four servants? The Japanese housewife then depended almost completely on servants for cleaning, washing, cooking, tidying up, and minding the children. When Japanese housewives got together, complaints about the boy and the amah were rife. They pilfered and ate on the job, cheated on the change from the shopping, were lazy, and so on and so on.

Many of the boys and amahs were hostile or resentful toward the Japanese. Undoubtedly they also felt envious of the opulence of the lives the Japanese led. However, even under such circumstances, a great number of Chinese were honest workers. Of course, since the Japanese had forced their way into China, the relations between Japanese and Chinese were not on an equal footing. There were some individual Japanese who were kind toward their Chinese servants. But, on the whole, the Japanese treated their Chinese servants as fools, had a preconceived view of them as inveterate liars and thieves, and looked on them with disdain. This was one of the things which bred anti-Japanese feelings among the Chinese.

So I bring this woman's letter to my class and comment in the following manner. There is a history of large circumstances, and within that there is a history of small individuals, like grains of rice. These two histories cross somewhere. They have points of contact. Though the individual may think the greater circumstance is irrelevant to himself, actually the individual is never unrelated to the greater circumstance. But how is that relationship made up?

When one considers the relationship between the greater circumstance and the individual in wartime, one thinks, for example, of how individual life and livelihood are destroyed by war. While this certainly cannot be overlooked, there is another consideration. The daily life of the individual, and within that his attitude and posture toward life, is in fact a remote cause of war itself, and it constitutes part of the forces that commence and sustain war. For example, how did each individual Japanese who crossed over to China before or during the war relate to the Chinese, and how did he treat the Chinese employed in his household? This sort of thing was certainly not unrelated to war. Of course, it was the imperial Japanese government which started the war. And the military, bureaucrats, financiers, industrialists, and rightists were the moving forces behind it. Yet it must be admitted that ordinary people too, in their everyday life, preserved the seeds of war, and fertilized them. War is not to be thought of only as that which destroys the everyday quality of the individual's life, since there is something in the everyday quality of people's lives that fertilizes the seeds of war.

Although there were good people among the Japanese living

in China at that time, in the eyes of the Chinese they were Japanese who had come to China as rulers, against the background of force exerted by the Great Japanese Empire. Their individual goodness coexisted with the aggression of the state. Within that coexistence, individual goodness sustains state aggression.

I think the point made by the woman criticizing the Japanese living in Indonesia is extremely important. Though it would be an exaggeration to say that those Japanese who treat Indonesians with disdain are nourishing the seeds of war (since it seems unlikely that present-day Japan could easily embark on an aggressive war), they are definitely sowing the seeds of poverty and adversity for the Indonesian people, as well as contributing to the sowing of the seeds of future difficulties (and possibly even catastrophe) for Japan.

It may be that among the friends of the families of the students listening to me there are some who happen to have gone to Southeast Asia. These students may well feel some disquiet over what I have to say. However, the tragic connection between individual and circumstance is not just a question of the former being crushed by the latter. It is tragic because so often the former fertilizes the latter. The life of Japanese in Indonesia is an issue of moment for the students. From my prewar experience I can imagine the life they lead. I cannot be indifferent when the same pattern develops now that did half a century ago when I spent my boyhood in China.

IV

I put before my students a poem by the Hiroshima poet Kurihara Sadako.

"Let the Child Be Born"

It is night in the basement of the collapsed building.

The wounded of the atomic bomb
Crammed in, filling the basement,
Not a single candle to light the darkness.
The smell of fresh blood, the stench of death.
Heat from sweaty bodies, groans,
And from the midst a strange cry is heard:
"A baby is going to be born."
In this basement like the depths of hell,
Now, a young woman has gone into labor.
Not a single match in the gloom,
What shall we do?
People grow considerate, forgetting their own pain.
"I am a midwife. Let me help with the delivery,"
Says one of the seriously wounded, who just now
    was groaning.
In the depths of this gloomy hell,
A new life is born.
But before the light of dawn the midwife,
Still stained with blood, dies.
Let the child be born,
Let the child be born,
Even if it means throwing away one's own life.

                     (1946)

    "Let the Child Be Born" is quite a famous poem, but nearly all my students say they have not read it. There are so many things in this poem that I want to discuss with my students.

    Kurihara Sadako was in Hiroshima when the atom bomb fell. She devoted herself to poems and literature about the bomb. This poem was published in the first issue of the journal *Chūgoku bungaku* in the year after the defeat in the war. She wrote the poem after hearing this story from another survivor. The girl who was born then has now grown up and lives in Hiroshima. My students look astonished when I tell them this.

    Of course I mention at this point that because the American

authorities had decided to preserve the secret of the atom bomb they immediately placed a total ban on the publication of reports, comments, or opinions about the blast. For example, I tell them about Shōda Shinoe's anthology of poems *Penance*, which was distributed as a kind of illegal publication. And I introduce some of Shōda's *tanka* poems. Or I tell them about Ōta Yōko's novel *Street of Corpses*, which only saw the light of day after very severe scrutiny by the Occupation Forces. Or I tell them about the photographs of the keloids of bomb victims, which were not shown to the public till 1951, six years after the bomb, when they were published by the *Asahi* newspaper. None of my students know any of these things.

There is no end to the topics that come up when we turn to discussing matters arising from Kurihara's poem: the course of the Second World War; the history of the construction of the atomic bomb; its completion and testing; and Hiroshima and Nagasaki; the havoc wrought by the bomb; the way in which it was reported at that time, both in Japan and overseas; who first reported it; and the occupation policy forbidding reports about the bomb. Above all, I tell them of the circumstances of the livelihood of innumerable nameless victims. Those who most needed relief were most neglected; not only that, but they were even discriminated against in their daily life. I speak about all of these things. Then I tell them how the victims of Minamata disease were discriminated against. In other words, at least I want to get across the fact that those who suffer as victims are also discriminated against—that remarkable double distress which occurs almost invariably, as if it were a sociological law.

Next, I present my students with a copy of "When We Say Hiroshima," which Kurihara Sadako wrote during the Vietnam War, twenty-six years after "Let the Child Be Born."

"When We Say Hiroshima"

When we say "Hiroshima,"

Can there be any gentle reply of
"Ah, Hiroshima"?

When we say "Hiroshima," the reply comes back,
   "Pearl Harbor."
When we say "Hiroshima," the reply comes back,
   "Nan-jing Massacre."
When we say "Hiroshima," the reply comes back,
"Women and children
Heaped into a ditch
Burned to death with gasoline in Manila."
When we say "Hiroshima,"
An echo comes back of blood and flames.

When we say "Hiroshima,"
There can be no gentle reply of
"Ah, Hiroshima."
The anger of the dead, of the voiceless people of Asia,
And of all against whom crimes were committed
Wells up
When we say "Hiroshima."
For there to be a gentle reply of
"Ah, Hiroshima,"
We must really reject
The weapons we should have rejected.
Foreign bases must be removed.
Till that day Hiroshima
Remains a city of cruelty and distrust,
A burning pariah.

When we say "Hiroshima,"
For there to be any gentle reply of
"Ah, Hiroshima,"
We
Must cleanse
Our sullied hands.
         (1972)

After reading to the end, I return to the first three lines.

> When we say "Hiroshima,"
> Can there be any gentle reply of
> "Ah, Hiroshima"?

These three lines: what do they point to in concrete terms? I try asking my students this, but the replies that come back never amount to much. This is because the students do not know enough about the history of the Fifteen-Year War and the barbarities committed during it by the Japanese army. For this reason alone, I cannot help being conscious of the shallowness of the "peace education" of modern junior-high and high schools. I take it on myself, therefore, to tell them concretely about Nanjing, Manila, and so on.

This poem of Kurihara's was written in 1972, during the lifetime of my students; it is indeed contemporary to them. I call to their attention the fact that in the period from 1946 to 1972, at the very least there was a great change in the war consciousness of the Japanese people and in their thirst for peace. That is to say, from the time the US forces began bombing North Vietnam in 1965, the realization was born within us that Japan was now standing in the position of aggressor in the Vietnam war. This realization brings us back again to our own experience as war aggressors, to prewar Japan and the attitude of the Japanese people of that time.

When defeat came, we felt almost as if we alone were war victims. Indeed, in relation to the military and the ruling strata, among whom the military figured, the Japanese people were war victims. But it was the Japanese people who had gone off one by one, rifle in hand, to invade China and other countries. And it was the people of China, the Philippines, and Indonesia who were the victims.

"Let the Child Be Born" is one of the most outstanding poems on the atomic bomb. Although it does not directly raise the question of the responsibility of the United States for the dropping of the bomb, Kurihara's husband, publisher of the magazine in which the poem appeared, was summoned by the Occupation Forces and given a very hard time. This occurred even though all the poem depicted was the tragedy of the bombing, and in the midst of the tragedy a young mother struggling to deliver her child and the midwife who died exhausted by the effort of assisting the delivery. However, the blending of life and death, and the birth of a new life surmounting death, make the poem a powerful hymn to life.

The mood of the poem "When We Say Hiroshima" is, in contrast, very bitter. This mood is conveyed in the poem by the renewed sense of the aggressive character of the Japanese state itself, twenty-seven years after the end of the war. It expresses the poet's anguish at seeing the rebirth of an aggressive Japanese state. Its message represents a terminal point in Japan's postwar history. By comparing these two poems, I ask the students to consider the significance of the twenty-seven years that elapsed between them.

Above all, I point out to the students that "When We Say Hiroshima" talks of their own age and their own generation. How the young read this poem is a key to how the young today interpret the present age.

V

I introduce my students to these two poems. Yet there is all sorts of material, literary and documentary, which symbolizes the three periods of modern Japanese history: the war, the period of militarism; postwar, the period of democracy (or quasi democracy); and contemporary Japan, the period of the triumph of economism resulting from high economic growth. Adults are in no position to hold the young in contempt just because they may be indifferent to the problem of war and peace, since adults themselves are submerged in the present age of economism and have lost all sense of tension with their times. I feel within myself that I want to speak about war and peace not out of duty but out of inner compulsion.

In precisely these circumstances, the demand that something be done about peace education is strengthening. Far be it from me to oppose such a demand. There are, however, few teachers who enthusiastically involve themselves in peace education, and the students, I hear, tend to be unresponsive. How can I help but feel apprehensive and sad? There is, in addition, something else. That is, do the teachers themselves feel an inner compulsion to speak to their pupils and students about the problem of peace? I think teachers must ask themselves this question.

It is a question to be asked regardless of whether or not one has experienced the war. If we assume provisionally that teachers who have what could be called war experience means those of over about fifty years of age, then they are a minority among teachers in Japan now. If experience of war is to be the criterion, then peace education is beyond the reach of the majority of teachers. But clearly peace education is not something of which only the wartime generation is capable. At the same time it is axiomatic that for the war generation to move into peace education, their own experience is an obvious starting point. Peace education can be carried out in various ways using varying materials. It is important only to look at what is in the heart of the teacher. The teacher cannot pass on to others something which he does not feel himself.

At a certain university there was a mathematics teacher who was approaching retirement. During the war, this man had been first a private, then a noncommissioned officer, then an officer, and he had gone to the war in China and taken part in some fierce battles. At this university, there was another teacher, this one in his forties. He knew that the old teacher approaching retirement was opposed to war. But he also knew that not once had that teacher ever raised the subject before his students. He urged the old teacher, before he retired, to speak of his war experience to his students. He not so much urged as pleaded with him.

At first the old teacher refused. He said he was a mathematics teacher, unqualified and unable to speak in the classroom about anything outside his specialty. However, the younger teacher eventually prevailed upon him to accept. The younger teacher also invited other students not taking his colleague's class. In this way the hour of the special lecture arrived.

The old teacher began haltingly. He mentioned lots of Chinese place names, and spoke of battles he had participated in. He spoke of the way his friends had been killed and injured in battle. And he also spoke of the ''enemy'' losses and how the Chinese people responded. Gradually, the old man's words came to life. The allotted lecture time of one and a half hours passed, but he spoke on. Not a single student moved. As he neared the end of his lecture, nearly three hours after he had begun, the old teacher became unable to restrain his tears. What had the war brought? Why had young people believed they had a duty to fight and gone off to the battlefield? What had the Japanese army done on the continent of China? What had the Chinese people suffered from the war? How had the Chinese, combatants and noncombatants, stood up to the Japanese army? When he finished, the students broke into loud applause.

Nowadays in all universities there is a fixed number of hours for general education, but much of it has become a formality. With this in mind, who would deny that the talk the old teacher gave was truly worthy of the name of general education?

▌▌▌ Chapter Three ▐▐▐

The War Inside Me

I

Qingdao was a beautiful town.

In the hinterland of Shandong Province two German missionaries were killed in 1897. The German government subsequently exercised strong pressure on imperial China and succeeded in obtaining a ninety-nine-year lease on an area around the superb natural harbor of Jiaozhou Bay. In its attempt to catch up with Britain and France, Germany thus established a foothold on Chinese territory.

Unlike Ji'nan, capital of Shandong, Qingdao figures little in the long history of China. There were only small fishing villages scattered here and there in the area. From these modest beginnings, all of a sudden a completely European town was born. The beauty of Qingdao was forged out of the original natural beauty of the spot and the rational spirit of the Germans.

When the First World War commenced in 1914, Japan—in accordance with the Anglo-Japanese Alliance—sent troops to Qingdao, which was in the possession of the German army. From this point onward the period of Japanese military rule starts. My family came to Qingdao during this period, and I was born in the Ōmura district of Qingdao City in 1917.

In my first childhood recollections Qingdao blends with the

Japanese military. This blending became the starting point of my thinking about the world.

Our family moved from Ōmura to the Ariake district. These place names were brought to China from the Japanese island of Kyushu and imposed on Qingdao by the Japanese military forces. At Ariake as a boy of five I used to stare at the top of a hill called Mount Kamio, which could be seen, all one hundred meters of it, from the front of our house. The hill was named after General Kamio who led the Japanese troops in the attack on Qingdao. At noon, when the characteristic sound of a cannon was heard, a puff of thick, white smoke appeared above the battery placement, gradually disappearing into the blue autumn sky. Soldiers who lived on the mountain used to fire one shot daily at noon—which the Japanese residents called "*don*"—as a time signal.

One day in 1922, however, the cannon fired what was to be its last "*don*." The Washington Treaty had come into force, and the Japanese army had to withdraw from Qingdao. Infantry troops with red epaulettes—privates as well as officers—walked away up the hill in front of our Ariake home. The sound of a bugle could be heard above the noise. Squeezing my mother's hand, I saw the soldiers off, my heart filled with sadness.

Not long afterward the name Ariake was abolished, and the street was called Longkou Lu. Japanese residents grumbled. They had forgotten that before they arrived all places in the town had German names. In only a little over half a century Qingdao changed hands about ten times. The Japanese had no experience of such a thing. First, the Germans came with their army. They were the first masters, and they were builders. Then the Japanese troops arrived, and Japanese military government was established. Later, military rule was changed into a Japanese civilian government. Japanese occupation ended in 1922, and their administration was taken over by a regional Chinese warlord faction affiliated with the Beiyang military clique. The leaders of this faction changed several times. Following the successful Northern Expedition of Chiang Kai-shek, Qingdao came under the sun-in-the-blue-sky flag of the Guomindang government. In 1938 Japan again occupied the town, and the Japanese remained virtual rulers, represented by a puppet Chinese administration, until the end of the war. After the war Qingdao was returned to the hands of the Guomindang government until, in 1949, the Chinese Communist army entered the town, to remain its master to the present day.

When rulers change so often, the citizens, willingly or not, develop a political consciousness. In Qingdao, it was not the Japanese, who lived under the protection of the government, but the dominated Chinese population, in particular the intellectuals, who developed considerable political sensitivity.

I may have watched the withdrawal of Japanese soldiers from Qingdao in 1922 with apprehension, but this was merely a reflection of the atmosphere within the Japanese community. In fact, the Japanese military forces did not leave after all. Instead of the army, the navy came to protect the Japanese. When I started going to primary school, for most of the year one or two Japanese warships were anchored offshore in Jiaozhou Bay or at the wharf in the harbor. Not only that, but once a year at the beginning of April, when schools were still on their spring vacation, Qingdao was visited by a combined squadron of the Japanese navy.

One year when I was at primary school, my father and my older brother took me to the top of the hill, from where we had a splendid view of Jiaozhou Bay, and we watched dozens of warships approaching. On the top of the hill were the remains of a fortress built by the Germans during their occupation of Qingdao. As I looked out seaward, the masts of the ships appeared as black spots on the horizon. Then the masts turned into a succession of vessels. It was a grand spectacle. After the battleships *Nagato* and *Mutsu*, cruisers, destroyers, submarines, and aircraft carriers formed a long line. We boys fought for the binoculars. The following two days were for us the "navy days." From what was called a navy pier we were allowed to inspect the warships. Or we could watch a *sumō* tournament put on by the sailors. The greatest pleasure, however, was to listen to a concert given by a naval band. Both my brother and I loved music, and, except for listening to a harmonica, this was the only opportunity we had during the year to hear a live musical performance. An overture, a waltz, an intermezzo, a march, extracts from operas, so the program went on, and it invariably closed with a naval march. When the cymbals provided the cheerful sound of clashing brass in the last refrain, I sighed sadly and was close to tears at the thought that it was all over.

And then, in the early summer of 1927, the first Shandong expedition took place. Under the pretext of defending the life and property of Japanese citizens who lived in Shandong Province, a large army detachment disembarked in Qingdao. I was in grade five of primary school at the time. For the accommodation of one or more army divisions, school facilities were not enough. Ten soldiers were billeted in our house. The reader can imagine how excited I was during these several days while "our soldiers" stayed. My mother treated them to meals such as *tenpura* and noodles, *sukiyaki*, and various dishes, inexpensive but delicious, made with beef or prawns. The soldiers too must have been delighted. But above all perhaps, I was carried away by the feeling that we had risen to the status of "patriotic family." The following year saw the second Shandong expedition. Chiang Kai-shek's army passed Ji'nan and proceeded northward. In order to "defend" Japanese residents from the strongly anti-Japanese army of the Guomindang government, Japanese army troops landed again in Qingdao. Earlier in the year there had been an incident in which a Japanese living in Ji'nan was killed by a group of Chinese. The Japanese and Chinese armies clashed, heavy fighting ensued in Ji'nan, and finally Chiang Kai-shek's troops withdrew from the city.

On the instruction of the Japanese consulate-general, children from the upper grades of primary school and from the junior high school went to the wharf with little flags to welcome the troops whenever a ship arrived. From our house it took almost an hour, but I considered it to be the duty of a patriotic child to go and never played truant.

A Japanese child could walk alone through deserted streets without ever being beaten up by the Chinese or attacked by Chinese children. When I think about it now, it seems almost unbelievable. However, at that time, no such danger existed because "our soldiers" were there.

II

In 1931 the Manchurian Incident took place. I was in the final year of junior high school.

My father was an avid reader of the journal *Nihon oyobi nihonjin* (Japan and the Japanese). This journal, in which Miyake Setsurei was involved, became famous for its ultranationalistic position. However, it also maintained an antibureaucratic stance, and in a way there was something noble about it. After the Marco Polo Bridge Incident, this journal developed into a fanatic partisan of the Imperial Way.

When my older brother started attending a university in Tokyo, he came in contact with left-wing thinking and urged our father to read journals such as *Chūō kōron* (Central Review) and *Kaizō* (Reconstruction). These journals began to appear on my father's shelves alongside *Nihon oyobi nihonjin*.

Nevertheless, I was a more enthusiastic reader than my father. The *Second Story of Poverty* by Dr. Kawakami Hajime was published as an appendix to *Kaizō* in 1930. I pounced on this. The book was a commentary on dialectic and historical materialism, and its style, filled with passionate, sincere emotion, was utterly enthralling to me. After entering university, I came to think that Dr. Kawakami's understanding of dialectical materialism was somewhat mistaken; at that time, however, the book was my bible.

One's view of society can change radically thanks to a single book. Such change may remain purely on the level of ideas; however, I tried to connect these ideas with the actual world. There was the semicolonial position of China, the reality of the invasion of China by the world powers, the shockingly low standard of living of the masses—for someone who lived in China, all this was so immediate it could be felt on one's skin. After my meeting with Marxism in the world of ideas, I suddenly lost all interest in the combined naval squadrons and no longer felt like going to listen to the military band. Looking back upon this time, it seems to me that I underwent what was perhaps an unnaturally sharp transformation.

After the Manchurian Incident, Japanese naval troops marched through the streets of Qingdao even more frequently than before. The Chinese looked on, in particular the young and the students. They watched with a cool detachment, with an expression which did not express anything. I could feel this attitude. I came to know it. On other occasions, the Chinese students would form columns and march past, chanting "Down with Japanese imperialism" to keep in step. Whenever I came across groups of students like this, I cast my eyes down.

I was accepted by a higher school in Tokyo and from then on I used to spend only the summer in Qingdao with my parents.

On 7 July 1937, the day of the Marco Polo Bridge Incident, I was in a third-class cabin on board a Japanese passenger ship sailing from Moji, Kyushu, to Qingdao. We learned about the incident from handbills distributed to the passengers after the news had been received by telegraph. In one corner of the third-class cabin young people argued in agitated but hushed voices. They were Chinese students studying at Japanese universities. When I went up on deck, a Chinese student who was studying at a private university in Tokyo came up to me and asked what I thought about the incident. After we had discussed the matter for some time, he told me in a low voice: "I'll not be going back to Tokyo in September. I must take part in the anti-Japanese war."

Later that year I contributed an article to a high school literary magazine. I wrote among other things that ''at present the Japanese are enthusiastically behaving as if Japan were deciding China's destiny. There is no doubt, however, that one day China will be determining Japan's fate.'' I was reprimanded, and the passage was deleted from my manuscript.

On board the ship I felt that for the Chinese students, as they themselves had said, there certainly was somewhere for them to go back to. But where was I returning to? To the ''comfort'' of our Qingdao house, a comfort provided for us by the brute strength of the Japanese state.

In 1971 I went to Paris and met an elderly Frenchman who was an enthusiastic campaigner in the anti–Vietnam War movement. When I mentioned in the course of our conversation that I was born in Qingdao in China, he immediately countered: ''And I was born in Algeria; my father was a colonialist.'' My memory was suddenly activated. Recollections flooded in, and we regaled each other with stories of our ''pleasant'' experiences in Qingdao and Algeria, as if each would outdo the other in the evils he had to reveal.

Human beings, whether in the form of states, races, or classes, are all too weak when faced with comfort. Few possess a moral drive strong enough for them voluntarily to renounce a life of comfort once they have experienced it. Nevertheless, some young Japanese, few though they were, and many young Chinese, did have such courage.

III

The year before the end of the war, I was working as a tutor in the Faculty of Arts of Tokyo Imperial University and was drafted from there to the Navy Technical Institute. Psychologists had been working in the institute for some time and now philosophers, sociologists, historians, literary scholars, and other specialists were mobilized as well. Why this was done I do not know. Anyway, quite a few of the intellectuals who were attached to the institute became extremely active after the war, and some of them later wrote about their experience.

Initially I worked as an assistant on various projects, including, I remember, one called "A Policy to Rouse the National Fighting Spirit." However, from about March 1945 things changed. We were told to express freely any suggestions we might have concerning the current situation. People in the top echelons of the navy were presumably looking secretly into ways to end the war.

At the time I retained a strong interest in developments in China and was reflecting on the question of how relations between Japan and China would unfold after the war. I believed that after the Second World War the Communists, from their base at Yan'an, would defeat the nationalists. This too was a conclusion based on my limited experience gained in Qingdao.

I requested permission to conduct an investigation into the Chinese Communist Party, and, for several months, until a few weeks before the end of the war, I was completely absorbed in these investigations. I was then twenty-eight years old. Already I had understood that Japan would be defeated in the war. In my diary I wrote: "This is a time when 'bravery' means to believe in victory because one is actually a coward."

Every day I walked through the fire-ravaged streets of Tokyo. I called on China specialists working for the universities and for the newspapers. From the research division of the Ministry of Greater East Asian Affairs I obtained on loan a translation of Mao Zedong's *A Theory of New Democracy* and Edgar Snow's *Red Star over China*. From Mr. O, the head of the Soviet section at the Ministry of Foreign Affairs, I heard a surprisingly accurate assessment of the developments that would occur in the world after Japan's defeat. After the war Mr. O campaigned against nuclear weapons and took part in the peace movement. In the underground shelter of the headquarters of the Navy General Staff deep under a hill in Hiyoshi southwest of

Tokyo, I met with Colonel H. In an annex of the General Staff located on the campus of Meiji University, a consultant named B told me that the Chinese Communist Party would come to control all of China after the war. These interviews were possible thanks to my position at the Navy Technical Institute. In the end, I boldly requested an opportunity to listen to the opinions of the jailed officials of the Japanese Communist Party. As I should have expected, this request was turned down. Instead, I began explaining my ideas to people I met. Most were astounded. But I noticed that as we went on talking, unexpectedly many agreed with me. Others, however, warned me solemnly. "Remember," they said, "that as a consultant to the navy you are defenseless against the military police of the army. It's a dangerous game!"

I could not give up halfway. Something deep inside was driving me on. I suppose I was obsessed with the question of the long-term postwar relationship between Japan and the rest of Asia. I formulated my opinion in writing,* knowing all too well that, realistically speaking, the issues I wrote about could not possibly be taken up. I was given an opportunity to present my report to a group of people. Among them was one admiral and, to my surprise, Professor Hiraizumi Kiyoshi of the Tokyo Imperial University. At the time my report must have sounded immoderate, perhaps even absurd. The general trend in the world, I said, is toward democracy. Japan should make the following declaration: all Japanese military forces and civilian personnel overseas (in Asia) will be repatriated. Claims over Korea and Taiwan will be surrendered. An international appeal will be made for the complete independence of India, Burma, Indochina, Indonesia, the Philippines, and all other Asian countries. The Japanese military will immediately hand back to China the territory of Hong Kong, which they are still occupying. Within Japan, absolute freedom of speech, assembly, and

---

*For the text of this memorandum, see appendix.

association and an eight-hour working day and other reforms will be implemented.

Apart from the occasional embellishments which I had to use under the circumstances at that time, the proposals were quite straightforward. Considering that they were presented within the military, the situation appears fantastic, perhaps even comical. Obviously there was no agent who could implement them; it was all too late, and anyway to bring them up at this forum was a mistake. It was quite the wrong place for a political proposal of this sort.

Professor Hiraizumi made a frontal attack. "You start from the world situation whereas we must start from the principles of Japanese national polity. An argument which puts the cart before the horse like this is utterly deplorable." Fear spread upward from my feet through my whole body. The professor had considerable influence with the military.

However, the pace of the war was quick. The only consequence of this incident was that at the beginning of August, a week or two before the surrender, I was dismissed from the Navy Technical Institute. The reason given was that my views were incompatible with those of the navy.

IV

Then as now, I sensed a certain ambiguity in my father's thought, an ambiguity which logically speaking was strange but which was not completely impossible to understand from a psychological point of view.

Chauvinism and good will, aggression and friendship coexisted in my father's mind. On the one hand he was an avid reader of *Nihon oyobi nihonjin*. On the other hand he always admonished us never to say *shinajin* [Chink] but to say *chūgokujin* [Chinese]. He lamented that the overseas agencies of the Ministry of Foreign Affairs, the cotton mills built by Japanese capital, and the Japanese army and navy were arrogant and oppressive toward the Chinese and completely lacked sincerity and good will. In particular, he lambasted the army and navy for the fact that even in their ranks there were people who were hunting for concessions. Once, when he formally complained about the case of a military man who had demanded money and goods from a Chinese citizen under threat, he was summoned by the military police and beaten up by a young lieutenant.

On the other hand, my father supported hard-line diplomacy against other nations, and firmly believed that Japan had to fight European and American imperialism. When the Pacific War started, he put a large map on the wall and daily drew a picture of the Japanese flag over newly occupied places. My father, who so genuinely regretted the rottenness of the Japanese military and civil personnel in occupied Qingdao, seemed never to imagine what was going on in those places which were beyond the reach of his eyes. Perhaps he expelled such ideas from his head because they were too painful.

An invading army is almost bound to be brutal. And colonialists are almost invariably selfish and overbearing. This can be seen to be historically inevitable. For someone within the system it is close to impossible to break loose. You are ordered by a superior to kill a civilian or to stab a prisoner. Even if you summon up courage in the face of certain punishment and refuse, there is always another soldier who will do it for you. The good will of an individual cannot change the brutality of an army of aggressors. But, though it may leave no mark on history, it cannot be said that there is no difference between the kindness of one and the brutality of another. The existence of people who lack the force to change history is not something devoid of meaning.

I would not like to be misunderstood here. My intention is certainly not to defend the aggressor or the colonialist. I have repeatedly spoken about the responsibility Japan bears for what happened in China. And even though nowadays it is true that the friendship between the Japanese and Chinese leaders is a conspicuous factor in bilateral relations, I believe as before that the question of accepting responsibility for aggression continues to be the most serious problem for Japanese intellectuals.

Japan's left-wing forces have been an important factor in shaping the face of postwar Japan. These forces at one time consisted of people who during the war were locked up in prison, those who were critical but remained silent, those who had been converted to support for the war but who early realized the error of their ways, and those who supported the policy of the state only to realize their foolishness after the war—the last being particularly numerous among the young.

During the war, I was more or less a member of the silent group. Had I been born some five or ten years earlier, I think that one day I would have come up against the Public Peace Preservation Law, and I am the sort of person who finally might have become a convert to the state ideology. My feeling that those who did not take any action, though they understood, were worse than those who supported the government without knowing what they were doing made me act with some reserve. At the same time I thought that within a human being there was always something that did not measure up to the standards set by the logic of historical inevitability.

After the war people often used to say things like, "Regardless of his subjective intentions, his objective role was. . . ." On the whole I accepted the correctness of this phrase, but I expected that somewhere the opposite should also be noted, that "regardless of his objective role, his subjective intention was. . .," and I considered this proviso important. In general an allowance such as this was rarely made in the heated atmosphere of the postwar leftist movement. Objective and subjective should be one. Yet in fact most Japanese people fell into the gap between the two. Many who possessed knowledge lacked courage. After a certain period, courage alone was no use. Among those who lacked knowledge there were some who possessed the desperate courage to join the "special attack" [kamikaze] units, but their actions could scarcely bear fruit.

More than anyone else it was the leaders who deserved criticism. Their subjective intent could not exempt them from responsibility. I believe that popular investigation into the extent of their responsibility after the war was insufficient. At a time when most people have become confused and lost track of the oneness of objective and subjective, it is easy to point out their ignorance, but it is never easy to rescue them from desperation. I wonder whether the democratic forces after the war have ever really succeeded in explaining the meaning, or lack of it, of the various "intentions" of those who did their level best during the war.

I think this means also that righteousness may sometimes conflict with compassion.

When righteousness and compassion combine, people are moved. When compassion is absent under the flag of justice, people keep their distance, at best feeling some respect. It is appalling when the great cause of justice turns out actually to be unjust. And even when the cause is just, so much the more must there be compassion. Yet compassion alone, needless to say, leads self as well as others into unhappiness. Compassion may be described simply as the recognition that man has but a limited existence. It is impossible to understand man in his entirety unless one understands both his capacity for righteousness and for compassion. And, without understanding man in his entirety, it is difficult to find any clue to his total liberation.

One day, after the war had ended, the writer Noma Hiroshi and I were walking through the streets of Hongō in Tokyo, where simple shacks were beginning to rise on the debris of the air raid fires. I was reflecting that the liberation of man must extend through all dimensions: biological, psychological, and social. Noma was planning a comprehensive novel to develop exactly these same thoughts.

V

After the war I heard from those who had been repatriated from China that a new expression, *"can sheng"* (tragic victory), had been coined there to describe the situation at that time—after the sacrifices of the long war with Japan, and as the civil war between the nationalists and the communists was beginning.

For the Japanese, defeat in the war was undoubtedly a great blow, but when I think about it now it seems to me that, compared with the "tragic victory" of the Chinese, it might even be described as a "comfortable defeat." Of course, for those who saw hell itself in the Battle of Okinawa, the atomic bombs, or the air raids, the phrase "comfortable defeat" could not possibly seem appropriate. However, we must not forget that the countryside of Japan, where one half of the country's population lived, did not become a battlefield. For this reason alone, there can be no comparison with the Chinese countryside, which was exposed to the strategy of "burn all, kill all, loot all."

The per capita national income of Japan is now the highest of all Asian nations. It is more than twice that of Singapore, four-and-a-half times more than Taiwan's, seven times that of Korea, ten times that of the Philippines, eleven times that of Indonesia, and fifteen times that of India. The reasons behind the postwar economic revival of Japan are complex. One factor was that the high prewar level of development of industry, technology, politics, and education had a decisive effect in the postwar period too. In the same way as in other advanced imperialist countries, these standards were built up on the basis of the possession of colonies, and, in the case of Japan in particular, on the basis of policies of military aggression.

In present terms, it is undeniable that Japan's economic expansion in Asia and other countries contains elements of economic aggression and causes the destruction of local national industries. In the past we saw the military aggression of the Great Japanese Empire, and when it was routed it reappeared in a new guise. How does this seem to other Asians, especially since the economic growth of the 1950s and 1960s was achieved through exploitation of the Korean and Vietnam wars?

The report of the secretary-general of the International Labor Organization (ILO) to the organization's fifty-sixth general assembly, held in June 1971 in Geneva, contains a statement to the effect that unless attempts at reducing differences of wealth within individual countries are successful, it will be difficult to make a positive contribution to reducing the gap between different nations. The secretary-general of the World Federation of Trade Unions, present at the meeting, had words of praise for the report and expressed his satisfaction. While not wishing to impugn the ILO, I cannot help feeling uneasy at the idea contained in this statement. The economic gap between the countries of the South and those of the North, far from narrowing, is actually increasing. Can the masses in the so-called developing nations, whose average income remains one-tenth of that of workers in the developed countries, wait until differences in wealth within the developed capitalist countries disappear? I am afraid they will grow impatient and explode. Indeed, they are exploding already.

Soon after the war a professor of French literature whom I highly respect wrote that while Japan was lucky not to have become a battlefield, he was afraid that as a result the Japanese might quickly forget the war and court a new disaster. People who once carried out the policies of Japanese colonialism are now the political leaders of Japan. It is difficult to imagine that they could comprehend the sufferings of the masses of the colonial countries who have been continuously oppressed and discriminated against by them. Of course, the Japanese people who selected these political leaders cannot evade responsibility. And this situation is not unconnected with the fact that the majority of us, even after 15 August 1945, still do not understand the suffering of the people of our former colonies.

It is because the memories of China and of war live so strongly in my mind that I think in this way.

IIII Chapter Four IIII

The Age of "Neglect of the Public and Indulgence of the Self"

I

Each year as 15 August draws near, newspapers and television programs are flooded with reports and commentaries on the significance of the date. And each year one hears how this observance is being drained of its content and becoming more of a ritual. The Fifteen-Year War, the Japanese military's aggression against Asia, the dropping of the atomic bombs, the defeat, the years of poverty, the swing toward democratization that followed, and the promulgation of the new constitution—all these things transpired. But the memory of them is gradually fading away. Besides this, the number of people for whom all these events are past history is ever increasing. It is in this context that one hears comments on how well the observance has "weathered."

I was twenty-eight years old on 15 August 1945. As someone who belongs to the war generation, I am critical of this tendency. At the same time, I realize there is no point in just deploring it; we must develop a new approach, a new consciousness.

I am of the view that an extremely important qualitative transformation has occurred in Japan during the third of a century which has passed since the day of defeat in the Second World War. Fifteenth August 1945 was a moment of visible and dramatic change. But when I talk about qualitative transformation I am referring to those changes which took place around 1960 and which were prosaic and very difficult to perceive. If I am asked to weigh the comparative importance of the two types of change, I would be tempted, as a member of the war generation, to answer that 15 August 1945 was the more crucial. But for those who were born around this date and are now in their thirties or forties, what I call the prosaic changes may have more significance.

What kind of changes were these? Japan became one of the world's leading economic powers. As a consequence, it entered into a state of conflict and contradiction with the countries of the Third World, especially those of Asia, as well as a state of competition with the advanced capitalist countries.

Let me try to define some periods within the last sixty years of Japanese history, bearing in mind my own personal history. I was born in 1917. The years after the First World War are referred to commonly as the period of Taishō democracy.* This period can be said to have lasted until 1931, when the Manchurian Incident occurred. At the beginning of the Shōwa years, in the late 1920s, Marxist literature was widely read by Japanese intellectuals. Radical liberals and Marxists shared a common antipathy for militarism and fascism. Around 1931, I aligned myself with this view and held quietly to it until the day of the end of the Second World War. Japan as a whole underwent rapid militarization, especially after 1931. This militarization was eventually to lead to collapse.

With defeat in 1945 and its aftermath, Japan was subject to enormous external pressure. Pressure ''from below,'' from intellectuals and from the mass of the people, existed too, but unfortunately the situation was such that this alone could not bring about the democratization of Japan. Still, there was an overall

---

*The period of responsible party government and of liberal and democratic trends between the end of the First World War and approximately 1931.— Trans.

consensus of opinion within the country with regard to national goals. No matter how poor and small a nation Japan might be, internationally it should abide by pacifism, and domestically it should build a democratic society where meager resources would be equally shared.

It was from around 1960 that, for a combination of reasons, Japan began to take the course of high economic growth, a process so precipitous that Japan has now become the third strongest economic power in the world.

On the basis of these considerations, the sixty years of my life can be divided into four phases: the period of Taishō democracy, the period of militarism, the period of "democracy" or quasi democracy following defeat in the war, and the period of economism. I put the word democracy in quotation marks to indicate that democracy was not fully implemented despite the propagation of the new constitution and the other efforts made to democratize Japanese society. In the first period too, the period of Taishō democracy, both the framework of the nation and the consciousness of the mass of the people revolved around the emperor. In this sense, there is a strong continuity between the first and the second periods. By way of contrast, the discontinuity between the fifteen years of war and the postwar period is obvious (though one should take note of the more subtle points of continuity). On the other hand, between the period immediately after the war and that from 1960 to the present, aspects of continuity are obvious while aspects of discontinuity are not so easy to detect. It is this qualitative change, difficult to detect as it is, which I would like to examine next.

II

How have the Japanese people oriented their lives for the last half century?

There is one particularly valuable set of data given in the table presented here. The Institute of Statistical and Mathematical

Studies, which was established after the war, has conducted nationwide opinion surveys on the "national character" every five years since 1953. The table covers the period through 1978. I find the data valuable because they include one item which remained unchanged from prewar surveys. Through this material we are able to trace trends in the orientation of the Japanese people over a span of fifty years.

THE MOST CONGENIAL LIFE STYLE
(unit: percentage)

	1930	1940	1953	1958	1963	1968	1973	1978
To do what you find interesting, regardless of money or honor (Interests)	12	5	21	27	30	32	39	39
To lead an easy life in a happy-go-lucky fashion (Comfort)	4	1	11	18	19	20	23	22
To work hard and make money (Wealth)	19	9	15	17	17	17	14	14
To lead a pure and upright life, resisting the injustices of the world (Propriety)	33	41	29	23	18	17	11	11
To live a life devoted entirely to society without thought of self (Civic Spirit)	24	30	10	6	6	6	5	7
To study seriously and establish a reputation (Honor)	9	5	6	3	4	3	3	2

Note: figures may not add up to 100 due to rounding off.

The prewar surveys were conducted by Professor Toda Teizō, my own teacher and mentor, in 1930 and 1940, using for his survey young men being examined for conscription. When the professor told us about the surveys, I happened to ask him if answers to the questions might not represent *tatemae* (socially accepted norms) rather than *honne* (one's true inclinations), since the survey was conducted at the conscription test center. As I remember it, Professor Toda admitted this possibility but maintained that a certain degree of objectivity was assured since the respondents remained anonymous.

At any rate, the same questions were asked in each of the surveys from 1930 to 1978. To the best of my knowledge, these are the only available surveys on people's attitudes that are consistent over a period of time. The phrases in parentheses in the table such as "interests," "comfort," and "wealth" are categories set out in a book entitled *An Illustrated History of Postwar Public Opinion*, published by the Opinion Survey Research Institute of NHK (the Japan Broadcasting Corporation). The categories were not included in the questionnaires.

To summarize the general trends that these surveys reveal, there are no major changes throughout these years in regard to people's attitudes toward "wealth" and "honor." Changes are most evident in the other four areas. Concerning "interests" and "comfort," the level first declines from 1930 to 1940, but after the war it rises rapidly. Supposing these two categories can be treated together as belonging to the sphere of private life, then I think we can say that the categories "propriety" and "civic spirit" belong to the sphere of public life. In 1940, six percent gave priority to "interests" and "comfort" and seventy-one percent to "propriety" and "civic spirit." By contrast, the 1978 survey shows the first two at sixty-one percent and the latter two at eighteen percent. The year 1958 marks the changeover, and the beginning of what I call the period of economism.

In the words of the *Illustrated History of Postwar Public Opinion*, the Japanese in recent years have become "inclined to attach more importance to the individual than to society and to enjoy the present. They prefer to live in a nuclear family group, and they aim at high education as a basis for a stable private life. These tendencies became conspicuous in the postwar years, promoting and strengthening the way of thinking which gives priority to 'private life.' "

I think this description is accurate.

III

From "sacrifice of the self in service to the state" to "indulgence of the self, neglect of the public"—in this simplified way I often talk to young people about the transformation of the consciousness of the Japanese from the prewar to postwar periods. Simplification can, of course, sometimes be misleading.

I then elaborate on my statements. Immediately after the war, people were infuriated by the principle of "sacrifice of the self in service to the state," for this was the very principle that had led eventually to tragedy. As a result, the young totally ignored the prewar slogan and plunged into "indulgence of the self, neglect of the public"—the ethic of the black market. At the same time, there appeared a new form of "sacrifice of the self in service to the state." Sacrifice was redirected from the special attack [kamikaze] unit to the Communist Party. I tell my students about Tokuda Kyūichi, the Communist leader released from prison after the war, who used to write "selfless devotion" when his supporters asked for his autograph. I explain that I can understand the sentiments of those young ex-kamikaze pilots who joined the Communist Party. But young people nowadays find it difficult to comprehend the idea of selfless devotion, while the ethics of the black market are not beyond their imagination.

Just after the war, "from premodern to modern" became a slogan. Radical liberals advocated the importance of the "establishment of individual freedom." The leaders of reformist parties and labor unions—most of whom were Marxists—proclaimed the "rights of workers." Both the advocates of individual freedom and of workers' rights were deeply involved in political issues. It was a period of politics. Peace, democracy, improvement of the standard of living, and—after the occupation policies had begun to embrace the logic of the Cold War—independence. These were the ideals which had the power to move people to action and they were political in inspiration.

The notions of the "private" and the "public," reinterpreted, should have been integrated into the concepts of "individual freedom" and "rights." They were substantially different from the contemporary attitude of "priority of private life," which is in turn an adjunct of political apathy. What then was the force, the catalyst which transformed "establishment of individual freedom" and "rights of workers" into the "priority of private life" of today? The most significant agent in this transformation, it strikes me, was high economic growth and the concomitant change in life styles. But we must not forget the increasing number of nuclear families, the increase in the years of schooling, and the expanding influence of mass media culture—all factors which have often been mentioned.

Together with these developments, we must consider some of the key issues in postwar philosophical and ideological debate. First of all, we should note that the call issued after the war by liberals and Marxists for the establishment of individual freedom and the rights of workers was within the tradition of modernism embraced by Japanese intellectuals since the Meiji Restoration, in the sense that most of their arguments used the West as Japan's model. This is not to deny the existence of a handful of liberals and Marxists who went beyond this line of thought. Nevertheless, just as the opening of the country to foreigners at the time of the Meiji Restoration was accompanied by the anti-Buddhist, pro-Western movement, so, with the opening of the country after the Second World War, there was a wave of internationalism. Some members of the intellectual elite in postwar Japan went so far as to maintain that everything Japanese, in other words, everything indigenous, must be discarded. Thus this Japanese postwar democracy which revered individual self-reliance turned out to have been developed within the context of Euro-American political thought.

Another crucial point was that, especially for Marxists, socialism was the firm political objective. In the shadows of the ruins of war, the young were strongly attracted to socialist ideals. The view was commonly propagated that these ideals had already been achieved with spectacular success in the Soviet Union. I am not writing this from a naively anti-Communist point of view. I disagree with those who discard the thesis that the Russian and Chinese revolutions were inevitable occurrences. At least some of their subsequent accomplishments are worthy of attention. However, it has become clear during the last thirty years that there are numerous contradictions in established socialist countries. Awareness of these contradictions is more acute among the younger generation.

However, a qualitative change in the consciousness of the Japanese is taking place at a level much more profound than philosophical and ideological debate. Most Japanese now desire to maintain and expand their present modes of life generated by high economic growth. While many contend that the Japanese value system has diversified, the range of choices affecting style of life are limited. They are limited, for instance, to the question of whether to use one's bonus for the down payment on a family car, for an overseas trip, or for savings. In the sense that there is a determination to maintain and expand existing standards of living and life styles, values have been standardized, not diversified, and these standardized values have penetrated into the depths of our consciousness.

During the term of the Miki cabinet in the mid seventies, theories about life cycles proliferated. At that time, I had occasion to read one life cycle schedule that had been drawn up by a large labor union in the private sector. The plan saw workers through graduation from high school and the search for employment to retirement. It included such items as what durable consumer goods were necessary, when to purchase a house (on loan, of course), when to marry, how many children to raise, how many years of schooling these children should be given, and how to secure one's living after retirement. The schedule was drawn up on the premise that Japanese capitalism would remain in good shape for at least the next half century—no economic crises, no large-scale bankruptcies. But what is the aim of it all? It is this: that even shop-floor workers should be able to enjoy living standards comparable with section managers. The first impulse may be to laugh, but I find nothing funny about this labor union version of life cycle planning. It shows how deeply the desire for a comfortable life has penetrated into our psyche.

IV

That is why I call this the age of economism.

There would be no need to use this term if we were referring only to changes in industrial structure and to high economic growth. I use it to denote a situation in which the tendency to give priority to economic values strikes deeply into the individual consciousness of each citizen and affects his daily life style. It is, therefore, insufficient to define the current situation in Japan simply in terms of the restoration of militarism. A majority of Japanese do not believe in militarism. What we are observing today would be better described as a drift toward the status of great military power.

Some people have said—rightly, in my opinion—that the Ikeda cabinet, which was formed in 1960 after the demonstrations against the Security Treaty between Japan and the United States, effected a switch from the reign of politics to the reign of economics. However, economics in this sense is merely a tool of the politicians. To understand the substance of this argument, it is unnecessary to show the degree of change in the economic capacity and life styles of the Japanese between the immediate postwar years and the present. Any Japanese who lived during these two periods can grasp the point at once. The number of family cars on the roads nowadays, for example, is something the Japanese of the period before and immediately after the Second World War could never even have imagined.

There has been much talk recently of a swing to the right. While a certain drift in this direction is discernible, it would be quite wrong to associate it with the prewar brand of rightism. Problems do exist—the new requirement, for example, that the calendar year be numbered according to reign period, or the legitimacy of the present national anthem, or the government's support for Yasukuni Shrine, dedicated to the souls of the war dead. I was, and am, opposed to the rise of rightism of this type. However, it is necessary to appreciate that such means of political integration have considerably less weight now than they had in prewar years. It could only be by some very circuitous route that a contemporary youngster, a member of the generation for whom the "private life" has priority, could make up his mind to devote himself to the emperor. It would be an extremely difficult task of political manipulation to bring about such a transformation. Most probably, new political currents would have to be established. For example, it might become possible to orient the masses toward a new type of totalitarianism by emphasizing a philosophy in which it was not just money or comfort which constituted the aim of life. It is hard to tell to what extent symbols of prewar nationalism such as the numbering of years according to the emperor's reign or the national anthem *"Kimigayo"* could be used to pave the way for the propagation of this kind of philosophy.

One thing, however, is certain, and that is the existence of the demand to raise living standards. This demand is hard for any politician, whether conservative or reformist, to oppose. During the war years, the slogan "We will do without until we win" was used as a tool to effect political unity. Today, no matter who is in power, they have to deal with the reality of the fact that the overwhelming majority of the people put their private life first. But is it possible to reconcile the centripetal forces of political integration with the centrifugal forces of private enjoyment? In their attempts to reconcile these two forces, the programs of the various political parties resemble each other very closely. On the surface, this process appears perfectly democratic. However, it is inevitable that the difficulties posed by putting economic considerations before all else will some day have to be faced, particularly as endless increases in GNP and infinite improvements in the standard of living are impossible.

One would have to be an incurable optimist to believe that because "sacrifice of the self in service to the state" once destroyed the nation, "indulgence of the self, neglect of the public" will give rise to a bright future for the people. If the first is antihuman, the second is no longer human. I believe that unrestrained self-indulgence will result in a highly perilous state of affairs. (Incidentally, it should be said that a section of those who tow the self-indulgence line tend to be consciously critical of the status quo. Similarly, those who withhold their support from political parties are not perforce politically apathetic; some of them are expressing criticism.)

V

The philosophy of putting economic considerations before all else has brought three fundamental issues to the fore.

First, it has destroyed the relationship between human beings and the natural environment. The ecological cycle has been upset. We have already reached the point where the problem of pollution is so serious as to call into question the direction of our civilization.

Secondly, economism has destroyed the fabric of relations between human beings. People rarely use any yardstick other than profit and loss. Attitudes to life which are based on the principle of mutual assistance have been growing consistently weaker.

Thirdly, economism has given rise to both manifest and latent contradictions between Japan on the one hand and developing nations, particularly Asian countries, on the other. This third problem is perhaps the most important and the hardest to solve, but a solution is essential for the future of Japan in particular and for the world in general. Both reformist parties and labor unions have been reluctant to take up this point as a serious issue. For obvious reasons the same reluctance is shared by the Japanese government. But once we can appreciate this issue we realize why, since about 1960, Japan has been an economic power. Nevertheless, people have cast the issue out of their minds as though it were the plague. They have avoided considering the fact that the staggering improvement in their living standard is based on the sacrifices of the people of developing nations.

At the moment, the world is made up of one billion people who are overfed and three billion who are starving. This confrontation has been forged over the last few centuries. Political independence has not brought about economic betterment. This will be a cause of global turmoil in the future. How much time will have to elapse before some balance can be brought about between the two worlds? Our fate depends almost entirely on whether a transition can be peacefully achieved.

It is not that I regard the North-South problem as the only issue we face. It would not be easy to overlook the confrontation between East and West. Some have argued that the "democratization" of capitalist societies or their transformation to socialism would solve the North-South problem. And yet it should be sufficient to recall the Sino-Soviet confrontation and the conflict in Indochina in order to realize how fierce is the nationalism of socialist countries.

It is perhaps inevitable that the three billion people suffering from hunger will gradually reject advanced industrial nations if these nations attempt to further expand their industrial capacity, if they continue to waste natural resources and pursue the ideal of a comfortable life.

By and large, there have been three responses to these circumstances in Japan. First, the government and the ruling Liberal Democratic Party emphasize the significance of saving natural resources and reducing energy consumption but, at the same time, believe it is unavoidable that the economically weak will have to suffer, perhaps even to a considerable degree. There will undoubtedly be more calls for frugality and austerity. The weakness of such an approach lies in the very fact that it cannot be based on the principle of egalitarianism.

Secondly, reformist political parties and labor unions will presumably continue to demand improvements in living standards, wage increases, and various institutional reforms. Of course these demands will be intertwined with egalitarian claims. However, especially for unionists, the key question is what kind of equality they can guarantee for unorganized workers, part-time workers, and temporary workers.

Thirdly, though very marginal, some citizens' movements have begun to advocate a position that goes beyond the framework of economism. The slogan "Better to have pickled plums under a blue sky than beef in the smog" is one candid expression of this view. A small labor union recently formulated eight codes of action, the eighth of which was the statement "Be plain and simple." Implicit in this, of course, is a criticism of the substantial inequality which exists between unionists in large corporations and unorganized workers. There is also strong criticism of the massive economic disparity which exists between peoples of advanced industrial nations and the masses of the Third World.

How will the "frugality" and "austerity" which the government and the Liberal Democratic Party are certain to advocate strongly in the future differ from the "simplicity" referred to by some of the small unions? That is an important question, the answer to which we have yet to discover.

At any rate, these are the three ways of tackling the problems presented by the age of economism: "austerity" as advocated by the government and the ruling Liberal Democratic Party, "improvement in the standard of living" as argued by labor unions and reformist parties, and "simplicity" as formulated by a section of the labor movement and activists in the antipollution movement.

Just after the war, the catchwords peace and democracy had great strategic significance. So they do today. However, I cannot help feeling that new catchwords such as livelihood, life style, and culture (in reference to life style) have gained strategic ground. This they have done because the current economism, which assigns priority to one's private life, constitutes an important political tool.

A white paper on the national economy issued by the Economic Planning Agency several years ago already contained the phrase "quality of life." Facing a situation in which the philosophy of economism first can no longer sustain itself, the government has cleverly mobilized the masses not only by stirring up patriotism through warnings of danger to the good ship Japan but also by bandying about such catchwords as culture and the quality of life. Interestingly, the recent major slogans of the General Council of Trade Unions (Sōhyō) include the "struggle for culture and education" and the "struggle for women workers." Here, the "struggle for culture and education" is defined as the struggle "to consciously uplift the quality of life to a more human level." Further, Sōhyō says that "the practical objective under current Japanese circumstances is to 'attach greater importance to the enrichment of livelihood than to increases in production.' "

I have no idea what concrete proposals and implementation programs they have in mind when the government and the Liberal Democratic Party speak of "culture" and the "quality of life," nor quite what Sōhyō means by "enrichment of livelihood." Nevertheless, there would have been little question of this type of proposal ever being raised immediately after the war. Times are changing, and I am afraid they are moving in a contentious direction.

It is indicative of the character of our present situation that culture and livelihood constitute strategic considerations. Control is most manifest in these spheres. Nowadays, culture and livelihood are things provided from above or from outside. The citizen is provided with culture, education, and livelihood, all of it from off his employer's plate. Consumption, information, entertainment, and leisure are also all provided. Passivity in these areas is conducive to political passivity. What buttresses middle-class consciousness and motivates it toward economic considerations is the fear which many people have of losing what has been provided for them. They fear that the loss would mean collapse into lower social strata.

I am of the opinion that the age of economism will last a long time yet. It has generated among the Japanese, especially young Japanese, a life style which gives preference to private life. I was surprised to hear a student in my course say, "For young people today, freedom means having money and being able to buy things." He was speaking critically, I remember, but he identified with that attitude. For the Liberal Democratic Party bosses and the business leaders who call themselves patriots, this student's comment would certainly come as an unpleasant surprise. On the other hand, there is some irony in the fact that it is these same leaders who have cultivated in today's youngsters just such an attitude toward life. No doubt it would be difficult too for the leaders of reformist political parties and labor unions to accept the words of this student. However, it would be no easier for them to deny the connection between the overemphasis on the struggle for wage increases and the dominance of economic considerations. How, I wonder, will this broad base of young people, who embarrass both conservatives and reformists alike, react when it is realized that current stagflation is likely to continue for some time to come?

In the meantime, both conservative and anticonservative intellectuals and politicians have begun to talk about decentralization, about fostering a sense of community and regional feeling. These notions are nothing but responses to the crises and the chaos brought about by economism. Did anyone raise the idea of "community" in positive terms just after the war? Did anyone raise the question of the earth's natural resources and the ecological cycle at that time? At the very time when economism dominates and its difficulties have become visible, these concepts have been brought forward in order to effect some amendments to the path of development, or in the interests of a fundamental transformation of values.

From "sacrifice of the self in service to the state" to "indulgence of the self, neglect of the public"—this is simply one aspect of the change in the popular consciousness in postwar years. But it is, I believe, a change of great importance. I accept neither of these two orientations. We now need to embrace values different from either of them, regardless of the difficulty involved in nurturing these values.

|||■ Chapter Five ■||

The Trend Toward a Controlled Society

I

Everywhere in newspapers and magazines we come upon references to "the eighties," and among the eighties we find the year 1984.

It was in 1948 that George Orwell, sick with tuberculosis, completed his novel *Nineteen Eighty-Four*, which was published the following year. Orwell died suddenly of a lung hemorrhage in January 1950, at the age of forty-six. He had, of course, hit upon the title *Nineteen Eighty-Four* by reversing the last two digits of the year 1948. In that year he was fighting for his life in a hospital, and I feel sure the thought occurred to him that if he was still alive in 1984 he would then be eighty. The novel, which was published during the height of the Cold War, received much praise and much criticism too, but it was little understood. It appeared at a time likely to enhance its sales, but whether this was the best of times for appreciating the meaning of the book is a different matter. However, for Orwell, who was to die two years later, this was a last chance.

To remove at least some of the misconceptions about Orwell, I would like to introduce here a passage from one of his letters. On 16 November 1949, Orwell wrote in the following terms to a leading member of a federation of automobile workers' unions:

> My recent novel is NOT intended as an attack on Socialism or on the British Labour Party (of which I am a supporter) but as a show-up of the perversions to which a centralised economy is liable and which have already been partly realized in Communism and Fascism. . . . The scene of the book is laid in Britain in order to emphasise that the English-speaking races are not innately better than anyone else and that totalitarianism, *if not fought against*, could triumph anywhere. *

It was in 1950 that I first read the translation of *Nineteen Eighty-Four* by Yoshida Ken'ichi and Takiguchi Naotarō.† I can still remember as if it were only yesterday the feelings of terror, the turbulent and complex emotions I experienced, when I finished reading the book.

But what would Orwell have felt had he actually lived to see the year 1984? Orwell was of course painting a picture in *Nineteen Eighty-Four* of an extreme anti-utopia in an authoritarian world, but we have found out in the years from 1948 to the present that many situations similar to that depicted in *Nineteen Eighty-Four* have actually existed in various places around the world. They can be found in the Far East, Southeast Asia, the Middle East, Africa, and Latin America. They can be found too in the socialist bloc. Even in places where dictatorships have not become institutionalized—in Europe, America, and Japan—many individual examples can be given of human rights being trampled on by authority.

Orwell's fears are still alive today, and we can be sure that

---

*Extract from letter to Francis A. Henson in *The Collected Essays, Journalism and Letters of George Orwell*, vol. 4, *In Front of Your Nose, 1945–1950*, London, Secker & Warburg, 1968, p. 502.

†Tokyo, Bungei Shunjū Shinsha, 1950.

Nineteen Eighty-Four will once again become a topic of conversation in 1984.

Orwell died in 1950, and just one generation, thirty years, has elapsed since then. To those of us who have lived through these thirty years, things may seem to have been rather dull, but I see it as a period of great historical change. Different people would point to different things: to the various nations which have become independent—our neighbor, China, was liberated, and the impact of nationalism was felt in the newly emerging nations; to the diversification of social values—socialism underwent a reappraisal, and a North-South axis emerged in addition to the East-West one; to the rapid progress in science, technology, and industry—including the development of the hydrogen bomb, man-made satellites, travel to the moon, urbanization and industrialization with at the same time the beginnings of large-scale destruction of our ecosystem.

Orwell himself put forward three predictions for the postwar world. The first was that the United States would start a war with the Soviet Union—a preventive war—while it enjoyed a monopoly of atomic weapons. His second was that, during the Cold War, as a result of the proliferation of nuclear weapons in the hands of the Soviet Union and four or five other nations and the outbreak of a nuclear war, the civilization of the machine age would come to an end. His third forecast, which is of the most interest here, I cite in Orwell's own words:

> The fear inspired by the atomic bomb and other weapons yet to come will be so great that everyone will refrain from using them. This seems to me the worst possibility of all. It would mean the division of the world among two or three vast super-states, unable to conquer one another and unable to be overthrown by any internal rebellion.

In such states, Orwell believes that the anti-utopia of *Nineteen Eighty-Four* would become dominant. "Civilisations of this type might remain static for thousands of years."*

The novel *Nineteen Eighty-Four* has as its plot the crushing of a single citizen, Winston, by the party leader, O'Brien, for holding to an extremely insignificant heresy, but what is particularly distinctive is the confrontation between *omnipotent authority* and *absolute powerlessness*, with the difference in power being almost immeasurable. The means that O'Brien has at his disposal are infinite, ranging from physical torture to psychological insult. Winston is nothing more than the prisoner in Room 101 who is under total surveillance, both mental and physical. Control here reaches its utmost limits.

However, does control in the modern world always take this form? Certainly in the control techniques of Orwell's anti-utopia, it is not possible to exclude torture—probably the basest form of human behavior. But control that includes torture loses its effectiveness with the appearance of an opposition comprised of people who can endure the pain of torture. This can be seen both in South Korea and in Iran under the Shah.

I once read a highly interesting report by a special correspondent of the *Mainichi* newspaper (the Kansai evening edition of 8 February 1978). It was an account of a visit to the Seventh Physical Training School in Romania.

At the World Gymnastics Championships held in the United States shortly before the article appeared, the Romanian women's team placed first, ahead of the Soviet Union. The Romanian gymnasts had been trained at the Seventh Physical Training School.

This school, one of whose pupils was Nadia Comaneci, is located in the town of Deva in the western part of the country. Girls attending the school may be any age between six and eighteen. Students are chosen from all over the country by teachers and coaches. Members of the public are also invited to apply, and competition is so fierce that out of twelve thousand applicants only fifty are selected.

---

*Orwell, "Toward European Unity," op. cit., p. 371.

Once selected, the students are accommodated in dormitories, and strenuous gymnastic training commences. According to the headmaster, the age most suited to gymnastics is between fourteen and eighteen, and he is confident that a second Comaneci will emerge.

The best people available in the fields of gymnastics, medicine, physiology, dietetics, psychology, and pedagogy are employed at the school. We may be sure that the highest degree of scientific control is practiced there.

The correspondent had his doubts. The school channeled all its energy into gold medals at the Olympics and the world championships, and it seemed to him to be no more than a "factory for training champions" through the thorough implementation of a controlled regime of physical education. Yet both the headmaster and the local Communist leadership took a tremendous pride in the place.

While I have a certain sympathy for Romania as a socialist state following an independent line and not siding with the Soviet Union, I cannot help feeling that this sort of education is very odd. However, with gymnastics becoming increasingly acrobatic and competitive, it may be that the only way to win is to receive the sort of training the Seventh Physical Training School dispenses. This is a symbol of the times.

The training there is certainly not commensurate with control exercised through torture. In a sense it could perhaps even be referred to as control through education, even perhaps a humane type of control. I suppose it is quite likely that careful provision is made so the girls have games to ease their psychological tension and spare time to break the monotony of their daily lives. This would be done with the cooperation and under the direction of their psychiatrists. But would all this be done for the sake of their development as human beings or as an essential element in their training as gymnasts? That is the problem.

Needless to say, those who do not do well have to leave the school. The *Mainichi* correspondent described the sorry figure cut by parents and children, baggage packed, leaving the school. Furthermore, entrants to the school could scarcely be permitted to raise objections to the school's educational policy. It would be absolutely astounding if strife were to occur at the school.

This philosophy of control has the power to spread beyond national borders. If I were a conservative politician hostile to socialism, I would no doubt denounce this strictly regimented method of training champions as an extension of the conditions described in *Nineteen Eighty-Four*. However, I am sure that the leaders of Japan's conservative sports establishment would be interested primarily in establishing a national consensus on the need for an institute where future champions capable of competing against the products of the Seventh Physical Training School could be trained.

Thus the outlook of the leaders of Japan's sports world and of those in other areas who support them on the one hand and the philosophy of the leaders of socialist countries on the other are remarkably similar.

Orwell's *Nineteen Eighty-Four* and Romania's Seventh Physical Training School are by no means the same. Yet neither are they completely different. When they are examined at the same time, the differences are discernible only to the most discriminating eye.

II

Once, in 1953 so far as I recall, when I was on the staff of Tokyo University, I tried to find out in an end-of-year examination the views of my students on the subject of nationalism and national stereotypes. I introduced three topics: first, a quotation from *The Way of the Subject* (*Shinmin no michi*), a text which was imposed upon citizens by the Japanese government during the Fifteen-Year War; next, a passage from Hitler's *Mein Kampf*; and lastly, a speech by former senator McCarthy, infamous launcher of the ferocious witch hunt for "reds" in the so-called

Un-American Activities Committee of the US Congress at the beginning of the 1950s. I asked my students to analyze the characteristics of and the differences between Japanese, German, and American nationalism. I still remember how interesting in their own way the answers were.

State control under emperor-system fascism crowned by an imperial house ruling for ages eternal; the Nazi race principle appealing to German race, blood, and soil; and the principle of "freedom," blind even to the collapse of the cardinal principle of the defense of freedom and democracy and its subsidence into the negation of freedom—even now, consideration of the process of historical growth and the actual political functioning of such systems is a topic of inexhaustible interest. To this could no doubt be added a consideration of the different forms nationalism takes in different countries, those of East and West, and in the countries of the Third World.

In Japan's case, however, there are growing grounds for concern that strong feelings of nationalism might emerge again in the 1980s. People have begun suggesting that the Japan of the eighties bears similarities to Japan in the thirties, half a century before. Especially since the Liberal Democratic Party's overwhelming victory in the double election in 1980, it has been hard to ignore the increasing military orientation of the LDP administration. Soon after the inauguration of the Suzuki cabinet, there was talk of convening a comprehensive security conference, and thereafter the newspapers were plastered with reports of the build-up of Japan's defense capacity. It seems now that everything—politics, economics, industry, education—is being run with this "comprehensive security" in mind.

If present trends continue, it is possible that, excluding nuclear weapons, Japan, which is now seventh, will be the fourth largest military power by the nineties, behind the United States, the Soviet Union, and China. One thinks of the prewar Japanese empire, which used to be referred to as the world's fifth, or sometimes its third, greatest power. But, ironically, probably because the United States wants it that way, it is unlikely that Japan will ever have its own nuclear weapons. The United States remains extremely guarded on this matter. To arm itself with nuclear weapons, Japan would probably have to scrap the Security Treaty with the United States. In strategic terms, Japan is still subordinate to the United States.

It should be noted in passing that, in this process of militarization, the Security Treaty is being exploited to the hilt. The late Prime Minister Ōhira's parting present was the promise, made while in the United States, to strengthen Japan's capacity to defend itself. As a result of the Security Treaty, Japan has been made to provide bases, increase its defense capacity, and cooperate economically. The provision of bases is clear-cut; no need for comment there. The United States government has skillfully forged a connection between its demands for increased economic cooperation and an increased military capacity on Japan's part. If the Japanese government holds back on American demands of one kind, then as a *quid pro quo* it is confronted with even stronger demands of the other. For example, if Japan seeks a relaxation of export restrictions on Japanese goods, it is faced with a strong demand to increase its defense capacity. The reverse also holds good. Japanese business can reap a double reward by pushing for an increased defense capacity and in return secure economic cooperation from the Americans in the form of a relaxation of import controls. It is natural, therefore, that business should claim to see the strengthening of Japan's military capability as the most prudent path open to the country. Japan has certainly been making leaps and bounds down this path.

I for one could never bring myself to approve of this tendency. Is an opinion such as mine held only by an insignificant minority? I think not. Anxiety and apprehension are spreading. Already even the big newspapers, whose circulation is counted in millions, are sounding warnings about Japan becoming a great military power. For example, take an editorial that appeared in the *Asahi* newspaper on 15 August 1980:

> The government and the Liberal Democratic Party
> are stressing love of country and clamoring for a
> strengthening of the Security Treaty and defense. The
> business world too is vociferous in its support.
> Moves over the past few months have reached an
> exceptionally high pitch. At the same time, National
> Foundation Day, the law stipulating that years should
> be numbered according to the emperor's reign, the
> placing of Yasukuni Shrine under state protection, and
> various measures for the reconstruction of a social con-
> sciousness are being carried steadily forward. The
> future shape of things likely to develop from a pro-
> longation of these trends is ominous.

Another editorial, this one in the *Mainichi* newspaper, reads:

> Certainly a war of this nature [Second World War]
> did not happen all of a sudden. . . . Like a fatal illness,
> there are frequent preliminary warning signs, and the
> matter advances step by step. A decisive situation
> results if these symptoms are ignored. By then, even
> if one realizes what is happening, it is too late. Why,
> therefore, are we unable to cope in these situations?

The Japan of the thirties is being recalled as a lesson in both
of these editorials. The writers of these editorials were not thinking of Japan in the eighties as being identical to Japan in the
thirties; the problem is how they differ.

III

A comparison between Japan in the thirties and Japan in the
eighties is a comparison between prewar Japan and postwar

Japan. In between stands 1945 and defeat.

It would be a major task to consider and to analyze one by one the points of continuity and discontinuity in prewar and postwar Japan. To do so would mean examining the world of politics and of economics, social events and changes in the pattern of life.

It would not, however, be enough just to trace the continuities and discontinuities within each of these separate spheres. The important thing is to look at the whole structure within which they are brought together. In attempting this task, I would like to consider three dimensions: first, the internal organization of Japan; secondly, foreign relations; and thirdly, the consciousness of the people. All three, of course, are interrelated.

1. *Japan's Internal Organization.* The basic framework of Japanese society is the capitalist system. At the beginning of the Meiji era (1868–1912), Japan adopted the slogan "enrich the country, strengthen the army." In the thirties in particular, the army took the initiative and invaded China in an effort to solve Japan's internal economic problems, particularly those of unemployment and scarcity of resources.

After defeat in the war the policy of "enrich the country, strengthen the army" was abandoned; so, even more pronouncedly, was that of "strengthen the army, enrich the country." Such slogans were abandoned not only as ideas but also as reality. They were out of the question for Japan, a defeated country.

Any recovery after that had to start with "enrich the country," and from the beginning of the sixties there was a rapid revival. Japan became an economic power. "Strengthen the military" proceeded at a comparatively gentle pace. Nevertheless there is no knowing when it might take off like a startled rabbit.

For the time being, "strengthen the military" is pursued under the leadership of the business world. It is therefore oriented more toward economic gain than the country's defense or the protection of overseas interests. This is of course in spite of the fact that the strengthening of Japan's Self-Defense Forces has a quite different significance for American global strategy.

2. *Foreign Relations*. There are, in this world, those nations that are a nuisance or a threat to other nations, and those that are not. Japan has in the past both invaded and economically dominated other countries. From the point of view of those other countries, Japan's defeat in 1945 put an end to the menace that it had presented.

From the beginning of the sixties the Japanese economy once again began to wield power, to expand into developing countries and draw profits from them. Actual economic aggression commenced, and since then Japan has once again become a nuisance to other countries. There is a great difference between countries that are not a nuisance, countries that are, and countries that have the potential for becoming a nuisance. Such a difference is also reflected in the internal organization of countries.

3. *The Consciousness of the People*. As I have already noted, there has been a shift in the consciousness of the people from the sacrifice of the self in service to the state typical of the prewar years to the indulgence of the self and neglect of the public of the present day. Whatever sense of communal consciousness is left serves as a means for the preservation of private livelihood. The principle of owning one's own home remains undisputed even at the level of publicly acknowledged value, and as inner conviction it is unshaken. Thus, the Japanese people are no longer treated as subjects by the government, as under the constitution of the Great Japanese Empire; under the constitution of the Japanese state, they have had to be made partners, and due attention has had to be paid to the improvement of their daily lives.

In order to integrate into society people bent on self-indulgence, postwar Japan has been advancing step by step in the direction of becoming a controlled society. That advance continues even now. Compared with the prewar method of integration, which relied exclusively on exhorting people to worship the emperor, integration of the masses now proceeds at least partially through recognition of their individual concerns. Before the war, emperor worship was in a sense merely a front, and there is a sense now in which the government is eager to cultivate a new national consciousness. However, the direction Japan is taking in the seventies and eighties is toward a controlled society characterized by integration through induced spontaneity (even if false spontaneity) rather than by coercive, authoritarian means.

IV

It was Marx who, in his analysis of class society, drew attention to the economic exploitation at the social base and political control in the superstructure. I should now like to expand on this by taking up the question of social control and the making of a controlled society.

The most extreme form of control may appear to be that described in *Nineteen Eighty-Four*. However, to political authorities with a degree of sophistication, *Nineteen Eighty-Four* methods seem clumsy. The authorities do not wield permanent control but are inclined to bring on themselves instability and confusion. Mass control is accomplished not by hard but by soft methods; it is not one-dimensional but many-sided and many-shaped. Control over life style, culture, education, and consciousness assume particular importance. Even among conservative politicians, centralized control alone is seen as inadequate, and notions of decentralization of power have arisen. When prime ministers talk of the age of culture or the age of regionalization, this is not just waffle.

The notion of the "flexible structure" and the "repressive tolerance" of power used to be much discussed. But the emphasis was still given over to the techniques of rule. Now we are saturated with concepts of the age of this or that, of culture itself, and of life styles. It is not enough to view contemporary society merely in terms of politics and economics.

Controlled society transcends so-called differences of system. Both capitalist and socialist societies advance along the path toward becoming controlled societies.

Here I will discuss only the general framework of techniques for effecting control in capitalist society.

First is the profit motive, and profit and loss are today tacitly considered to have become the measure of the age. Nor do the authorities take any positive steps to suppress this. Indeed, the masses are drawn into the power structure by the prospect of profit, whether small or substantial. The masses themselves expect to be bought.

In the latter half of the seventies we heard a lot about structural corruption. But the people believe they are seeing only the tip of the iceberg. The real problem with structural corruption is that most people suspect that the corruption which is not exposed is probably much greater than what is exposed. Structural corruption is not so much a matter of economic activity as a cultural problem. Of course the profit motive has now become more or less respectable; it is no longer something to discuss in dark places. The dispensation of vast sums in subsidies in connection with large-scale construction work is one example of this.

A ruling political party which has the capacity to distribute largesse to one-third of the population will be able to retain political power over a long period. With an abstention rate of one-third in elections to the House of Representatives, the votes of one-third of the electorate constitute a majority.

The second factor working to control our lives is the "ready-made" quality of our lives, culture, and education. The mass of the people are cocooned by a ready-made livelihood, a ready-made culture, and ready-made education. This ready-made quality is not felt to be disagreeable. There is no sense of compulsion in it. Women who follow fashion enjoy being dressed in the livery of "ready-made" fashion.

There is no doubt that the rapidly developed popularity of color television and the motor car was a great coup for business. Few people, however, feel they have been coerced into buying these products. They are, in fact, nice to have—convenient and very interesting. They have already become necessities of life, so much so that any political move to do away with them would almost certainly result in a popular uprising. So it is not merely a matter of the lives of the masses being manipulated by politicians and their politics, since the lives of the masses actually regulate certain aspects of politics. Thus we have the paradox of the controllers being controlled by those they control. However, it is the controllers who get to make the first moves.

Third is the preservation of discrimination and distinctions. There are, for example, the distinctions made on the basis of schools attended, and there is discrimination on grounds of sex, social status (e.g., against members of the *buraku* minority), race, and physical disability. It is unnecessary for me to point out again here that the use of discrimination and distinctions serves as a hidden technique of control, exploitation, and supervision. And the way in which they are used is becoming increasingly refined. However, the preservation of discrimination and distinctions is not necessarily directly linked to political control or economic exploitation.

Fourth is isolation and exclusion. Anyone who voices an objection to the system of control, either of the society or of the workplace, is shunted off the rails of profit enjoyment, either openly or by covert means. Such people are always a minority. The harsh expulsion of a minority acts as a warning to others. The labor unions and political parties who are aiming at the majority and are intent on power gradually lose the strength and the will to help these people. As a result such minorities become more and more isolated. They exist outside the system. When the voices raised in their support are reduced to an absolute minimum, then the reality of *Nineteen Eighty-Four* will be brought home to them. There has probably been no country, no matter how "civilized," where secret torture and murder and private lynching have not occurred in police detention centers or prisons in the years since the Second World War. And the unhappy fact is that, as this trend increases, outbursts of violence of various kinds occur in resistance.

Finally, of course, there is nationalism. The Seventh Physical Training School provides an example. There should be little need to explain why. There exists an abundance of material—more than enough to write a book let alone a paragraph—about all the strains of nationalism that exist in various countries.

It is not easy to criticize a controlled society when it profits the masses and provides fame and status to individuals. Some may argue that the Seventh Physical Training School goes too far. Others would say the preparations to enter elite universities in Japan, with all the cramming schools for examinations, are taken too far. But how to tell when one has crossed the borderline of excess? There would appear to be a subtle continuity.

This vagueness, the impossibility of delineating a clear border, helps in the creation of a controlled society. As a result of this vagueness, it is possible to avoid the criticism and censure which blatant political oppression and economic exploitation are inclined to cause. One would expect the society Orwell described in *Nineteen Eighty-Four* to be abhorrent to all. However, the principal of the Seventh Physical Training School, his face wreathed in smiles, is a man not lacking in human charm.

V

The vagueness of the borderline between "going too far" and "not going too far" is evident in language itself. The control of language is a feature of our times.

The Japan Teachers' Union, for example, has for a number of years proclaimed as one of its slogans, "Comprehensible lessons, a happy school." This implies a criticism of the conditions that create such problems as dropping out and lack of discipline, problems that can lead to suicide, and the moves toward a school control system. On the other hand, the Ministry of Education has adopted the slogan, "Perfect schooling without pressure." If the connection with the Japan Teachers' Union and the Ministry of Education were concealed, many Japanese would no doubt consider these both to be splendid slogans. Wiser parents might retort that they would like to know not just the slogans, but their content.

In the thirties, "militarist Japan" was an expression with favorable overtones, while liberalism and democracy, not to mention socialism, were all bad. Both the reality and the words were regarded in a quite different light from today.

After the war, peace, freedom, and democracy were words which could be qualified by both conservatism and reform. But what was meant by the words was another matter. The common denominator was the positive connotations with which each word was endowed. The conflict between the realities did not become a conflict between words. Rather, different views of reality competed for the same words. One possible explanation is that a shared basis emerged for the value system of the nation. But a contrary view is possible, that the vagueness of the words is used to conceal the conflict between the realities.

In the period after the signing of the San Francisco Peace Treaty in 1951, the late Professor Uehara Senroku spoke a great deal about peace, democracy, independence, and the betterment of life as being the national tasks of the Japanese people. Independence he included because he had the system predicated by the San Francisco treaty in mind.

Whenever members of reformist political parties or labor unionists of that time spoke, it was to stress these four themes. There was an inevitability about the use of these words, and there was conviction and passion in the way they were spoken.

However, the vague and loose use of words has now led to perceptions of reality becoming vague. For example, consider the following: The Self-Defense Forces must be strengthened in order to preserve peace. Legislation to preserve peace is important for the sake of democracy. An autonomous constitution must be established for the sake of independence. The assertion of rights must be moderated and labor and management should cooperate in order to achieve improved living standards.

So not only people but words too are controlled. The world has indeed become a complicated place.

VI

Using the word "complicated" here reminds me of the memoirs of Jean-Paul Sartre. Sartre recalled that at the time of the Nazi occupation of France the choice was very simple: this side or that, cooperation or resistance. To resist, courage was necessary. Yet the choice was clear-cut. Ten years after the war the situation had become complicated, and the choices too had become complicated.

People often refer to these words of Sartre. They realize that he had grasped accurately and realistically the relationship between objective situation and subjective choice both during and after the war.

We can now see that there was a short period after Japan's defeat in which the world did not seem at all complicated. In particular, the message of the so-called democratic organizations immediately after the war was clear and simple. The ultimate goal of these organizations was a socialist society. It was assumed that there was a historical inevitability about the transition from capitalism to socialism. The capitalist camp represented the forces of war; the socialist camp, the forces of peace.

But in the following thirty-five years the situation was to change greatly. There occurred events which no one would have dreamed of immediately after the war: Hungary in '56, the Sino-Soviet confrontation, Czechoslovakia in '68, the Indo-Chinese conflict, and the Soviet intervention in Afghanistan. Of course, the American war of aggression against Vietnam should also be mentioned here since this was a salutary lesson to supporters of the free world. Of these, the incidents involving the socialist countries in particular had a serious effect on the Japanese peace movement.

Immediately after Japan's defeat in 1945 there was a clear and simple perception of the situation and of the direction the reformist movement should take. However, if one persists in using simple logic in a changing situation, the argument becomes complex and difficult to understand. It was the conflict between the position of the Sōhyō trade union council and the Japan Socialist Party, which opposed all nuclear testing on the one hand, and that of the Japan Communist Party, which held that nuclear tests conducted by socialist countries were defensive in nature while those by capitalist (imperialist) countries were aggressive, on the other, that caused the 1963 split in the movement to ban atomic and hydrogen bombs. It was the leader of the ban-the-bomb movement, the late Yasui Iku, who said at the time that "the peace movement should be easily understood by the people."

The position on nuclear testing was one problem. A more basic problem probably was the need to advance easily understood arguments about socialism. I think it is wrong to regard the peace movement and the socialist movement as one and the same thing. The Socialist Party, the Communist Party, and the Sōhyō trade union council must each clarify their view of socialism if they are to win people over.

Somewhere in the argument that nuclear testing by socialist countries is defensive lies the theory of stages of historical development from capitalism to socialism. But have not people during the last thirty-five years learned hard lessons about the inherent contradiction in this argument between idea and reality?

Is there any yardstick to help us decide which is the more serious problem: the judgement by a Korean military tribunal that Kim Dae Jung should be completely deprived of his human right to freedom or the arrest and imprisonment of opposition intellectuals and politicians by socialist countries? There is no essential difference between the deprivation of freedom and the violation of human rights whether they occur in capitalist countries, socialist countries, or Third World dictatorships. It is not a case of deprivation of bourgeois democratic freedom or of loss of proletarian socialist freedom but purely and simply the loss of human freedom. Simple concept though this is, it touches the hearts of people who were born and grew up in complicated times. Without such simplicity how can it be possible to transcend the corruptions of contemporary capitalism and the contradictions of socialism?

Sartre spoke of complexity and simplicity. I do not think that complex logic is always superior to simple logic; nor do I think that the reverse is so. Within complex logic, instances of simplicity may be found, and vice versa. When doctrinaire simplicity is confronted with reality, it becomes difficult to comprehend and therefore transforms itself into complex argument. However, when one loses one's direction in a complex situation, generally the best thing to do is to revert to one's original intent, confirm one's ideas, establish one's ultimate objective, and renew one's stand based on simple logic.

Looking at things more analytically, when the situation is complex, we must strive to grasp the elements in their complexity while remaining as firmly as possible in contact with reality. However, when we move on to determine our objectives and decide upon a course of action, that is, when we come to determine our ideas and directions, it is best to be simple and clear. It has tended to be the case that, even though analysis of concrete situations has been accompanied by simplification, much of it formalistic and dogmatic, complex standards have dominated value judgments—for example, in the appraisal of nuclear testing. It strikes me, in other words, that in relation to ideas and directions we should respect *as natural law* man's pristine sense of values, while analysis of circumstances should be painstaking and should be conducted *historically*.

When I use the words "pristine sense of values," I recall Sartre's *The Final Conversation*. There, Sartre speaks of the various values—liberty, equality, fraternity, the "bourgeois-democratic values" adopted in the French Revolution—as true left-wing ideology, and of the three, in particular fraternity.

A disappointment perhaps? I do not think so. Sartre's reversion to liberty, equality, and fraternity sprang out of that simple, clear perspective which sees the predicament of Kim Dae Jung and political prisoners in socialist countries as equally serious violations of human dignity.

For several years now, I have been considering the case for a shift from "scientific socialism" to "utopian socialism." Of course, these terms have a symbolic meaning, and I am certainly not advocating a return to Owen, Saint-Simon, or Fourier. However, I think that within the rather denigrated idea of utopia, there was a simple strength in terms of ideas, a fertile imagination, an experimental mind, a fundamental sense of justice, and a gentleness of soul, as well as a variety of universal values and related sentiments. The early socialists, in an extremely simple way, fought against social inequality, injustice, economic poverty, the oppression of humanity, and the tyranny of the powerful. That resolve was taken up by both Marx and Engels.

Compared to the excessively refined logic of today's scientific socialism, how strong are the traces of fresh utopian socialism that remain in Marx!

VII

What are the great problems that we face today in the world?

To begin with, there are the contradictions of capitalist society. Next there are the contradictions of socialist society. Then there is the North-South problem. The ecological problem, too, is considerable: environmental pollution, depletion of resources, population explosion. The progress of science and technology has brought with it problems such as those created by genetic engineering. The problems spill over beyond existing structures.

The question of peace is a problem of such a major order that it embraces nationalism in the socialist states and the question of nuclear proliferation. There is also the progress of the trend toward a controlled society, a trend which transcends social systems, and the associated problem of human alienation.

If anyone had tried to stress this problem in the period immediately after the war, there is no doubt that he would have been branded an extreme reactionary. Now, changes have appeared within the framework of the problems. However, no solution has been forthcoming. We are compelled to navigate without charts. By nature, people fear change, and the trend toward conservatism and control is facilitated as a result.

Out of these problems, two stand out. First is the question of how to create a society of real freedom, equality, and fraternity based on the spontaneity and autonomy of the people and not just to replace a bureaucratic capitalist society with a bureaucratic socialist society. Second is the question of which of the two, the advanced capitalist countries or the advanced socialist countries, will be able to win the peaceful competition for a solution to problems of the ecology and to the North-South question. In 1959, Khrushchev visited the kitchen of an average American household and boasted that before long the Soviet state would be able to offer Soviet citizens even more wonderful kitchens. But what a pathetic form of competition between the systems this is; what a way this is to decide which is superior and which inferior! If only there were a different sort of competition, a competition to see which of the two blocs was the better able to provide protection of life and livelihood to the people of the South, who make up two-thirds of the world's population, and not by creating unnecessary demands among the people but by creating the wherewithal for life as a human being.

For this the people of the advanced nations will have to desist from waste and rediscover a new, more human direction for their life. For competition to have real meaning it must be peaceful; its aim must be to see which country can first halt the enormous and absurd waste on arms production, and how those savings can then be directed toward aid to the people of the South.

Is this a utopian fantasy? If so, then the outlook for mankind is bleak. Perhaps it is bleak. But that is no reason for adopting a realism that verges on the nihilistic.

Let us shift our attention to problems within Japan. The view has been put forward by Asukata Ichio, [former] chairman of the Japan Socialist Party, that the reality of Japan is a "controlled type of fascism" (*Outlook for the 1980s and Subjects for Reform*). He picked out the following three points: (1) restoration of people's rights; (2) independence and solidarity (participation, decentralization, self-government); (3) creation of peace. A grasp of the mechanism of control is essential, I too believe, to an understanding of present-day Japan. But what can we do to overcome this controlled society? The problem resides at a fundamental level. What are the thought processes behind Asukata's points?

He uses the words "independence" and "solidarity." Independence ultimately refers to the independence of the individual, while solidarity is something forged between independent individuals. But what of the relationship between independence and solidarity?

Independence and solidarity often stand pitted against each other. There is, therefore, a great significance in relating the two in this way, and all the more so if the tension latent in the relationship is used as a lever in the dynamics of the construction of a new society.

In his first point, Asukata uses the expression "restoration of people's rights." Until now, socialists have thought of revolution and liberation in a collective sense. The Chinese Communist

Party called for liberation of the nation, independence of the state, and revolution of the people. However, a restoration of people's rights involves perforce the individual. There can be no restoration of people's rights without restoration of the rights of the individual. Once we realize this is so, our line of reasoning comes to take a different course from that of the Japanese reformists of the postwar period.

Capitalist morality used once to be equated with individualist morality, and socialist morality with collectivist morality. We can only hope and presume, however, that individualism will outlive capitalism; indeed, it must outlive it. If it were not to, then socialist society, in the name of collectivism, would fall easy prey to the control of the bureaucrats. Independence and solidarity are of equal value.

The unity of workers has always been stressed as something to be defended, something very precious. Indeed, it is. However, at the same time, I should like to stress the importance of defending as precious the human rights of the individual worker. Just as it is necessary to protect human rights through unity, so it is necessary to prevent any transgression of human rights through that same unity.

When the question of decentralization is raised, it is always considered in political terms. Granted the great importance of this, there is no doubt that the basis on which a centralized political system is established is the industrial structure itself, whether it be monopoly capitalism or a centrally planned economy. Decentralization, therefore, must be more than political. Economic decentralization is an essential accompaniment. Self-reliance and autonomy in the lives of us all will be established as this process is extended.

Behind this question lie the various alternatives available to us in the remaining part of this century and the beginning of the next. Controlling these alternatives is the relationship between ecology and socialism, which itself may be conceived in a variety of forms. What developments should we hope for? A centralized, regulated administration shifting to a dispersed, decentralized, self-management type of socialist administration; the mass production system becoming a small-scale production system; the overcoming of the division of labor as a new goal; a significant shortening in working hours; shift from private automobiles to public transport; the beginning of a break-up of the large cities; a more general participation in agriculture; a reappraisal of our relationship with nature and a restoration of harmony to the relationship; a swing away from a centralized-culture orientation and toward regional cultures; elimination of the distinction between work and leisure; a fresh estimation of the skills of the people as something more important than those of specialists.

In these ways, we might be able to overcome the trend toward a controlled society and solve the problems of the ecology.

Whichever course is followed, it will not be restricted simply to decentralization and regionalism. This process ultimately enters the province of the independence of the individual. However, that independence turns upon itself and points toward a new kind of solidarity. Man cannot live by himself alone. Solidarity did not originate as a form of unity among workers but on the much more intimate level of unity within communes of family, friends, or neighbors. Such small-scale solidarity must not be ignored when discussing the solidarity of workers. I think it is for this reason that Sartre chose fraternity, together with liberty and equality, as his ultimate aspiration.

VIII

The postwar era in Japan has been built on a policy of "enriching the nation." Now that this process is complete, politicians are beginning to think about "strengthening the army." But to achieve this, society must first be regulated and controlled.

Editorials in the major newspapers express opposition to a renewed strengthening of the military. However, their opinion is to absolutely no avail. When even opinion carried by the prominent newspapers carries no sway, whatever is to be accomplished through the strength of the individual? But the present state of affairs is the result of control of popular opinion. The profit incentive, the preservation of discrimination, and the isolation of dissenters—all these are the products of calculated moves.

Immerse yourself in your own life. Dissenters, whether in the workplace or in the locality, are bound to be defeated. You, what do you choose?

At one time, the motive that gave impetus to reformists in Japan was the maintenance of living standards. Things have now reached the point, however, where this has become part of the political platform of the conservatives. Even the spokesmen of the emergent new forces of nationalism have adopted the protection of the people's livelihood as one of their slogans.

It is, therefore, more than just political control, economic exploitation, and social discrimination which hold society together in Japan today. It is the process of increasing control over our livelihood, control of education, standardization of culture, and passivity of thought, in short, the all-pervasive character of the ready-made which holds the whole framework together. The structure that has been provided is such that whoever advocates anything other than what has already been made for him will suffer reverses in his own life.

There are some who feel disquiet about Japan becoming a large military power, but they can be left alone. As long as they submit to the terms of the life—the education, culture, and thought patterns—that have been charted out for them, then the advocates of a militarily powerful Japan can sleep easily.

Conversely, in order for our criticism of Japan's growing military power to bite home, we must all have the will to destroy the web of control over our life, over our education, culture, and thought patterns. At the very least, we must desire not to remain imprisoned in it.

Some examples of what I mean: if parents could have stood back a little from the trends of the day when considering their children's education; if wives had been able to lead their own lives more independently from that of their husbands; if daughters had not followed fashions so keenly; if sons had had more say about what sort of school they were sent to; if teachers could have been a little more independent of the framework of educational administration; if members of labor unions could have acted not only when they were mobilized or ordered to move but had been able to build their own movement a little more positively; if political party members could have had their own proposals and opinions and methods of action and not just accepted the theories of their organization without question (granting, at the same time, the role of organization); if people had been that much more independent of all aspects of the ready-made life, if all this could have been achieved, the present state of Japan would be very different from what it is.

The movement toward solidarity in all its various dimensions proceeds on the basis of the independence of each individual. Regions establish their independence from the central culture and build solidarity within the region; schools become independent from the educational administration as a whole and build solidarity within individual schools; regional offices establish their independence from the central administration; regional industry establishes its independence from monopoly industry; and people in the regions create human solidarity. Labor unions become as independent as possible from the state and from industrial enterprises and build up a new internal solidarity. Regional branches of the labor unions abandon their habit of never acting without instructions from higher organs.

Thus resistance to control is necessary on all fronts, beginning with the individual and rising through the levels of locality, district, organizations, federations of organizations, and ultimately reaching the level of the state. Some sections of the people's movement have now adopted this orientation. Having often arisen independently of existing political parties and labor unions, they are developing solidarity while maintaining independence. This was one characteristic of the seventies. Where were the points of departure for these movements? They were in the self-conscious, autonomous individual involved in his daily struggles. It was from these seeds that the movements were born.

Will the strong, popular determination that we should not remain forever controlled develop on a mass level? Will there be a clarion call? And will people rally around? The solutions to all the problems depend on this.

In the eighties, with the exception of a few branches sprouting into the realm of *Nineteen Eighty-Four*, the main trunk of social change is likely to be in the direction of the Seventh Physical Training School. How will we react? Our times are times of great transition in the sense that we face and must overcome situations of a kind that man has never before experienced, and we must do this without having first exhausted the process of transition from capitalism to socialism. For this purpose, it is not only the solidarity of the workers, but also the autonomy of each individual and their linking and solidarity that is crucial. At the same time, we must not neglect a symbiotic relationship of great importance to us, that with nature. What is needed now is an ideology that enfolds all of these concerns and ties them to the wings of consciousness and imagination.

▌▌▌ Chapter Six ▌▌▌

On Youth

I

Recently I became acquainted with an Indian student who was born in Japan and had attended a Japanese primary school before moving on to English-speaking foreign schools here. On graduating from high school, she went abroad to an American university to study sociology. After entering the university there, she realized how little she knew about either her motherland, India, or her birthplace, Japan. To satisfy her interest she returned to Kyoto and attended lectures and classes in various subjects at several Japanese universities. Upon someone's recommendation she enrolled in my course on the history of postwar thought. To my surprise, the credit she received from me for the report she submitted at the end of the year on the atomic bombings in Japan was recognized as a unit credit by her American university. Is there any university anywhere in Japan which acknowledges course units on a reciprocal international basis without a formal bilateral agreement between the two universities to that effect?

That aside, the criticism this student had of Japanese students was scathing. It was specifically directed at the son and daughter of the family where she was boarding. "The daughter, a senior student at high school, is superhumanly immersed in cramming for examinations. Just how many hours of sleep can she possibly get every day? Yet her older brother who is at university studies incredibly little! He spends all his time playing. To me, they both seem to have lost their senses.''

She had grasped with astonishing accuracy the stereotype of today's high-school and university student. Of course, I know of university students, especially in the natural sciences, who are quite hard pressed by their studies. Yet students of disciplines such as law, literature, and economics spend on average probably only a fraction of the time on their studies that they had spent while at high school. If students graduating from my university were to take the First National Standard University Entrance Examination without prior preparation, their average scores would be far lower than those of candidates sitting for the exam. Indeed I even doubt whether the teaching staff at national and other public universities would do as well as candidates if they were to take the same exam. This alone indicates the absurdity of the National Standard Entrance Examination.

In Japan, the tendency is for entrance to university to be difficult and graduation easy. Some people believe that to remedy this situation entry should be made easy and graduation difficult; others, that university diplomas should be abolished altogether. At present, after a period of constraint and denial of freedom while a high school student, there comes a time as a university student when one is liberated from the trammels of cramming for examinations. Most enter university with the idea that now at last the spring of freedom can be tapped. Some, of course, expect to acquire higher learning at university. However, the content of most lectures at universities today is not of a sufficiently high standard to meet such expectations; nor does it really offer anything to satisfy the curiosity or imagination. It is highly revealing that university students see their student years as a kind of moratorium, a stay of execution granted them before becoming full-fledged members of society. How do they spend this period of reprieve? What do they think of this period of reprieve? What do they think is the correct way or the smart way to spend this time?

After graduation the great majority of them will go to work for a business company or become public employees. They will know that their stay of execution has come to an end. Some of them will become dedicated company men or women. Most will try to work at or above the average level and will do all they can to accommodate themselves to their organization. Criticism of the organization, or the harboring of doubts about it, is very rare; nor is such an attitude or such behavior tolerated. Daily work is seen as a means of making a living and the eyes are shut to any unpleasantness at work.

Thus, schematically speaking, "lack of freedom" as a high-school student is followed by "freedom" as a university student, and this is followed by "lack of freedom" as a member of society. Whatever can be the effect of such drastic changes in their environment on these young people? It is this which I believe to be the greatest single problem facing young people at university today (and more than forty percent of young people study at college).

Okamoto Seiichi, the first president of the college where I work, has created a unique tradition. "Freedom and Autonomy" is the school motto. The word freedom is constantly talked about. The students and, of course, the teaching staff are conscious of this.

At an April commencement ceremony, this young college president addressed his students as follows:

> You are already eighteen years old. This means you are adults by now. Under Japanese law, you may not vote until you are twenty, but I believe that to be a mistake in the system. There are other countries where eighteen-year-olds may vote. To be an adult means that one can think with one's own head, make one's own judgments, and have the right to freedom of ac-

tion. In that sense, you are free to do whatever you wish. I want you to be aware of the fact, however, that it is you yourselves who will be taking the responsibility for whatever happens as a result of your actions. Should you have any difficulties, the university will give you advice, but I want you to know that the university will not be taking responsibility for your actions.

I chuckled to myself when I first heard it. For a welcoming address before new students and their parents, this statement is forthright and unambiguous.

What is consistently lacking in Japanese education from nursery school through college is encouragement of the will to be self-reliant. There is a huge difference between true self-reliance and the mere posture of self-reliance. Those who emphasize the posture of self-reliance are critical of the attitude of presuming upon the tolerance and indulgence of others. But at the same time they stand for a sadistic spartan approach to education and so are the ones who repress the freedom sought by boys and girls and young men and women.

External conditions operate to repress true freedom and self-reliance, and in practice both are very remote from the grasp of young people. Responsibility undoubtedly lies with young people themselves. However, the external conditions that constrain the young today are much greater than adults realize.

There are quite a few universities which have declared ''freedom'' as their motto. Students enter these universities expecting things to be different from their high-school regime. It is no surprise if these young men and women experience at first a feeling of liberation. Freedom, however, is a great issue which confronts each individual; it is not something that can be resolved with mere slogans.

At the end of their first year, I asked the students in one of my classes to write their impressions of the year. One woman student wrote the following:

> There is indeed a certain kind of freedom to be found at this college. But to me it seems egocentric and uncaring. In the beginning, because I didn't grapple conscientiously with my studies, I thought I would be swept away. Since humans are weak, we are apt to let ourselves be carried along in the easiest direction. Surely this place should be more strict. Now I actually feel nostalgic for the strictness of my high-school days and wish those days would return. As things stand now, when I think about how I am going to spend the coming year, I become extremely uneasy.

Such impressions are far from unusual. In fact, there are many like it. The following impressions were written by another student and constitute a more moderate expression of the same view.

> This place is certainly free. The students are told to choose what they really want to study and what they really want to do. But as for myself, I don't *know* what I really want to do. Faced with "freedom," I feel completely *at a loss*.

There is yet another type of student. This is the student who, since coming to college, has learned that freedom means the ability to choose for oneself, to take part in a process of autonomous decision-making. Such students say that they have changed during the year. They take a critical view of their fellow students who hanker for a stricter regime. One student, a Korean resident in Japan, entered the college and selected Korean as her second foreign language. After a while, she suddenly dropped her adopted Japanese name and announced that she would henceforth use her Korean surname. The school of course welcomed this and the other students learned from the event. Many were deeply moved on reading what she had to say about her decision.

Another student, himself of *burakumin** origin, formed a study group on the *burakumin* and started a serious movement to investigate incidents of discrimination. Several other students, after attending a seminar on Minamata disease, decided to visit Minamata.† They then started activities to aid the victims of the disease. Another student, herself born in a farming village, conscious that the decision whether to return to the village and marry a local village man or stay in the city and marry a white-collar worker would represent a turning point in her life, decided to take up the study of Japanese villages and agriculture. In these ways the "freedom to do something," in other words, the *will* for freedom, develops among some of the students.

Freedom is something people long for. Yet the word "freedom" has all sorts of different meanings for university students who have suddenly been liberated from the restrictive regime of high school. There is insecurity and fear about freedom. There is bewilderment. There is unrestrained abandonment. And there is the will for freedom.

Along with this, there is also the type of student who adapts to the university, coping with the prescribed syllabus at the prescribed speed just as in high school, without joy or excitement, without any liberation of the imagination and without departing on any intellectual adventure. Such students are not even aware of the absence of true freedom. They are carried

---

*An outcast minority of people who were heavily discriminated against in traditional Japanese society and whose members still struggle for full liberation today. They number several millions.—Trans.

†Town in Kyushu, southwest Japan, which experienced mass poisoning from the effects of mercury waste discharged into the sea by a local chemical company. In the 1970s it became synonymous with the nationwide problem of pollution and the struggle to overcome it. For a detailed discussion, see Chapter Eight.—Trans.

along on the rails of the school, according to established patterns, unconcerned about whether they attain excellence or not. Such students are not bothered by illusions of freedom that may or may not exist at the university.

When those who had abandoned themselves without restraint to freedom or who were bewildered or rendered insecure by freedom while at the university graduate and enter the outside world, it is not at all surprising that they become either dedicated company men and women, loyal members of the white-collar army of the corporations, or obedient public servants. It is in this sort of phenomenon that we can detect a tendency to escape from freedom in modern Japan.

Life in the outside world is hard, not like student life, people often say. It seems that adults in general—like students before them—regard university life as a kind of stay of execution. People encourage students to enjoy student life. Yet most students feel insecure and bewildered in the face of all this free time or abandon themselves to it. As if they were laying secret psychological plans, students want to be liberated from this insecurity, bewilderment, and addiction. Not only are the young resigned to following rules and precedents obediently and not resisting authority, they actually regard these attitudes as positive.

The reason why a regulated society can function on the scale it does today is not simply a result of those in control being coercive or the technology of control being so advanced. Strange as it may seem, it is because the young people who are supposed to be seeking freedom spontaneously (this spontaneity is in any case false when considered in psychological terms) *want to be controlled.*

At high school, the elite sacrifice even their hours of sleep in order to devote all their energies to the study of the seven subjects designated in the five curricula covered by the entrance examination system. (Various competitive sports, including for example the high-school baseball tournament at Kōshien, are provided as a forum for the development of a competitive, devoted nature among the nonelite students.) These painful years behind them, they can relish the moment when they find out they have passed the entrance examination. Then, after four years of university life with its freedom that could somehow never quite be grasped, there begins again a life of regulations and conformity as a member of society. How can this possibly be enjoyable, even if, beyond this "pain," there lies the "joy" of a rise in status or the achievement of some work-related goal? It seems to me that it is the period of "freedom" during university days which actually helps to cultivate the disposition which sees pain and effort as one's inevitable lot.

If this nebulous freedom of university life were to become a habit carried over intact into one's working life with no correcting device, employers would fiercely denounce the universities. However, since employers know that even those students who lead the most irresponsible lives while at university become dedicated company men the moment they join a company, they have few complaints.

To a regulated society, an independent awareness of freedom and a clear commitment to freedom spell trouble. It would be a disrupting element in the contemporary social order if so many students with critical minds sprang out of the universities into the outside world.

The subtle changes of environment from restriction to freedom to restriction that accompany the transition from high school to university life and then to life in working society constitute a very ingeniously devised mechanism for the mass production of youths who will obediently conform to social regulations. If this mechanism was consciously devised, the person who planned and developed it was a master of control. I believe in fact that it was partly consciously planned and partly the incidental result of unplanned circumstances.

II

Let me talk about something very ordinary.

Anecdote One: I was invited one January day to attend a coming of age ceremony in a small town. They told me that they wanted me to say something to these "twenty-year-old adults." Brushing aside my doubts about the meaning of the coming of age ceremony, I decided it would be an interesting experience to meet these "adults," and so I accepted the invitation. Out of a total of about one hundred and twenty who were coming of age that year, sixty or so had gathered at the meeting hall, with about equal numbers of men and women present. To be honest, I was surprised. All thirty or so women who attended were dressed, without exception, in the most formal long-sleeved kimono.

Anecdote Two: Seven or eight women students about twenty years of age had gathered together. They were discussing women, and especially love, sex, and marriage. This is how their conversation went:

"If there is love, then sex is all right. Even if there is both love and sex, there is still no need to think of marriage (no objections, of course, if it leads to marriage). But romantic attachment and marriage are two separate things."

"There's no reason why people can't have sex even if they don't love each other. Sometimes love grows out of it; sometimes it doesn't."

"People marry, they have sex; out of this springs love. That sort of thing's not for me."

"Two people love each other. They get married; then they have sex. That's unnatural as well."

"If you fail in a love affair, it can't be helped, but for a marriage to fail is a dire matter. You've got to be clever about these things."

They were, on the whole, in agreement on these matters.

Now suppose that, at the commencement ceremony of a women's university, the college president were to give a verbatim account of this conversation. And suppose the president were to express complete agreement with the opinions of these students, in front of the parents sitting in the audience. It would probably provoke considerable criticism. It could only fail to create a stir if the college president were an excessively skillful rhetorician—or an extremely clumsy one.

If parents then were to voice complaints or differences of opinion, what would be their real intentions? They may indeed express surprise that students hold such opinions, or they may pretend to be surprised, but in reality I doubt they would be very shocked. What they would not want is that the school be seen to drop appearances. In other words, they would not want the critical eye of public opinion to be taken too lightly. It would not do to have it be said of the school that it instigated sexual liberation among its students. But no, the parents of these young women are not really worried. Their daughters all prefer anyway to wear the formal long-sleeved kimono. Furthermore, they are able to distinguish between a love affair and marriage. After graduating from love affairs, they will think carefully before making a choice about marriage.

For those young women who leave home to study in metropolitan areas, this period in their lives, separated from their parents, is indeed a stay of execution, a time of freedom. The students want it this way and so do their parents, who, despite surface denials, accept it somewhere in their hearts.

Before the war, parents did not tolerate their daughters having premarital sexual relations. Had a school teacher told his students in class that it was not necessary to adhere to such principles, he would most likely have been dismissed. The ideas of young women today on this matter are very different. One would be hard put to find a woman who felt guilty about having sexual relations with one man and then marrying another. Everyone more or less tacitly accepts this.

In this sense parents and daughters would appear to have changed greatly. But have they really changed? Before the war, if it were known that their daughters had "lost their virtue," that would constitute a severe handicap to their marriage prospects. At present both young men in particular and society in general are much more tolerant about this. Parents, therefore, are not as strict as they used to be. Behavior patterns have certainly changed. However, whether before the war or after, the attitude of parents has not changed as regards adhering to the trends and standards set by society. In other words, so long as one does not depart from the beaten path of society, everything is fine.

What is the beaten path? Society beats some very strange paths. For example, most parents would be shocked if their daughter were to announce that she was going to marry either a member of the socially downtrodden *burakumin* class or a Korean resident in Japan. Again, if parents learned that a young man's position and financial circumstances were insecure, that would provide a powerful argument for their opposition to the marriage. Or should the man in question be a member of what society calls the "radical movement," the parents would at once categorically oppose such a union. Yet these are times in which it is enough for young people to be involved in helping victims of Minamata disease or in the antinuclear-power movement for them to be labeled undesirables. Or, if a couple were to announce that they planned to live together but not marry, parents would probably be upset. Compared to these "barriers," the question of whether or not there is premarital sex is really quite minor.

Moreover, most young women would not dream of straying from the beaten path. Even if they experience sex and love, they will return to the tracks laid down by society. They believe that is in their interests. It is becoming increasingly common for women to come up with their own marriage partners before their parents have found anyone for them. Even then, a daughter will try to choose someone she expects her parents to approve. Most young women will put an end to a romance if they think their parents will not consent to the marriage.

I remember a conversation I once had with some women students. "When we go into a wedding hall," I said, "all we see are notices referring to the families that are party to a wedding. 'The Ōyama family and the Ono family,' they read, for example. But some say that it should refer to the people actually getting married, 'Ōyama Tarō and Ono Hanako,' let's say. What do you think?''

The students looked bewildered. Eventually one of them spoke.

''I think it best that a marriage receive the families' blessings. Why not have 'the Ōyama family and the Ono family'?''

Most of the other students agreed. It is now considered old-fashioned and lacking in style to read Article Twenty-Four* of the constitution at a wedding, although it was a popular thing to do for a time after the war. After all, this is the age of the formal kimono. And yet, in the final analysis, what does it all mean?

III

Before the war, about the time of the Manchurian Incident (1931) and the beginning of the Sino-Japanese war (1937), Turgenev's novel *Fathers and Sons* was published by Iwanami in one of their paperback series and enthusiastically read by a great number of young Japanese. The novel was always cited in discussions about the antagonism between generations. To the youth of Japan at that time, there was something deeply moving about the confrontation between a rural landlord and his son, a university student strongly drawn to revolutionary thought.

In Japan today, no more than one in a thousand university

---

*Article Twenty-Four: Marriage shall be based upon the mutual consent of both sexes, and it shall be maintained through mutual cooperation, with the equal rights of husband and wife as a basis.

With regard to the choice of spouse, property rights, inheritance, choice of domicile, divorce, and other matters pertaining to marriage and the family, laws shall be enacted from the standpoint of individual dignity and the essential equality of the sexes.

students reads the book. At one time, *Fathers and Sons* was considered a work that portrayed the eternal conflict of father and son, as if such a conflict would exist whenever and wherever.

Right after Japan's defeat in the war, those young people who had their wits about them all feverishly studied Marxism. About the time the Korean War started, I was teaching at Tokyo University, where many of the top students joined the Communist Party and participated in its activities. Protest movements were led entirely by these students. Most parents were deeply uneasy about this, but with the shock of defeat they had lost their confidence and were unable to control the behavior of their sons and daughters. So they let matters follow their own course. It could even be said that the parents felt there was something understandable about the ideas of the young.

From about the time of the struggle against revision of the Security Treaty with the United States in 1960, the number of Tokyo University graduates going on to become labor union secretaries or regional activists for the progressive political parties dwindled almost to zero. The winds of time changed. If by chance a youth showed an inclination to become involved in such activities, his or her parents would express their opposition in the strongest terms. As the economy entered its period of high growth, parents regained their confidence. Set speeches were devised to bring wayward sons and daughters back to the beaten track, speeches that began something like this: "Much as I appreciate the sincerity of your feelings, the world cannot be changed so easily." There were sporadic disputes of the *Fathers and Sons* variety at this time. Sporadic they may have been, but during the period from the 1960 Security Treaty struggle until the fall of Saigon and the end of the Vietnam War in 1975, tens of thousands of young people participated in mass meetings and demonstrations against the Vietnam War, against the construction of Tokyo's new international airport at Narita, on the Okinawa issue, and on university issues. Both then and now, I feel an affection for these students.

Inevitably, I did not always agree with these young people. Marxism was at the basis of their arguments, even the arguments of those who belonged to the anti-Communist Party factions. In Marxism, there is a framework of theory and practice. These young people held firmly to a belief in theory and practice, or they held firmly to the belief that they did so believe. Each political faction regarded the "correctness" (*tadashisa*) of its practice and the "wisdom" (*kashikosa*) of its theory as an exclusive possession. They would say that only in the beliefs of their own faction were correctness and wisdom to be found.

I told them often that I thought it difficult to win people over using only the conviction of their own correctness and wisdom. I suppose at such times they may have smiled derisively at me, dismissing what I said as the words of a person weak in the head, talking in his sleep. However, observing how punishment by expulsion led to purges and how interfactional violence led to the idea of mass murder, I felt there was some meaning in my position. And I wondered whether perhaps Marxism, while talking about correctness and wisdom, lacked a full appreciation of "gentleness" or "compassion" (*yasashisa*) and especially of the relationship between compassion and hatred.

However, from about 1975 on, the number of young people interested in the framework of *theory* and *practice* began to drop precipitously. There was at the same time an increase in the number of those who instead showed an allergic reaction to the very words Marxism and socialism. Lacking any framework within which to view the world or society as a whole, neither did they have the will to be active in or to influence society. It fell to me, a non-Marxist, to explain to students the greatness of Marx.

Recently the concept of "gentleness" has become popular among young people. One survey reported that young people valued gentleness above all other human values.

Gentleness here means no more than what it says. It has absolutely nothing to do with correctness or wisdom, theory or practice, referred to above. Rather, the way of gentleness involves breaking ties with such pretentiousness and setting aside grandiose postures. Politics, society, movements, groups—what point is there to it all? Even if there is no utopia to be found among Third World or capitalist countries, might there not be somewhere in the socialist world a country to be envied? So we arrive at a gentleness that bears absolutely no relation to political or other such realms. Even words like theory and practice, words which students thirty years ago heard so often they got sick of them—many young people today have not heard these words even once by the time they reach adulthood at twenty, or even by the time they graduate from university.

This gentleness is interchangeable with submissiveness. How very gentle and quiet the youth of today have become! "Correctness" and "wisdom" play no part in their lives, so what else have they besides gentleness?

When I was puzzling over the meaning of compassion, young people clung persistently to their notions of "correctness" and "wisdom." Now youth has lost all interest in correctness and wisdom and has become enslaved by gentleness. To adults, young people are no longer hostile beings. Adults no longer feel threatened by young people; they merely worry about them. They worry about their delinquency, their suicides, their neuroses. To adults, young people are not odious beings, rather they are beings who must be protected, guided, and gently brought back to the beaten path.

Because of the gap between generations, there are some things which are mutually incomprehensible. This is true about personal preferences, about matters of taste. However, neither adults nor young people regard the inability to understand each other in this area as a source of irritation. In the spirit of human kindness, where each side generously recognizes the other's viewpoint, that which cannot be understood is nevertheless tolerated. Both older and younger people have been able to understand each other better.

Adults have succeeded in turning antagonistic children into sensible children and adolescents. Those youths who cannot adapt take part no longer in protest demonstrations; instead they develop neuroses. Likewise, the manner in which they deviate has become more submissive. This submissiveness is different from that "compassion" which I considered earlier. There are, we know, youths who use violence in their homes or at school. However, I do not believe that these few delinquent youths are the main problem in society. I feel that the problem rather is presented by those youths who, within the given framework, are boundlessly submissive, boundlessly conformist. This is a pathological symptom of the malaise in our society today.

As regulations penetrate ever deeper into our society, the shadow of the antagonism between generations diminishes. Those who welcome this are unaware that hidden beneath their feet is a chasm that is spreading and expanding. Has it occurred to them to consider to what extent human beings can be controlled?

Adults are quietly amused to see the twenty-year-olds all dressed in formal kimono for the coming of age ceremony. The local mayor, the head of the board of education, the various leading figures of social education all likewise are dressed in full ceremonial attire. In this harmony of custom, the gap between the generations is nowhere to be seen. But is this cause for celebration and for peace of mind? Our "wisdom" can be gauged by how we answer.

Chapter Seven

The 19 April and 15 June Incidents

I

We sometimes refer to 1960 as the year of the Security Treaty. The struggle of April, May, and June of that year against the revision of the Japan-US Security Treaty, whatever else one may say about it, was the largest popular movement against authority and against the government in postwar Japan.

In April of the same year, what is known as the April Revolution occurred in South Korea—the 19 April incident and the collapse of Syngman Rhee's government. In Turkey too, on 28 April antigovernment demonstrations by students and others led to a change of government. Not that the incidents in these three countries were linked as a result of contact between the forces of the respective antigovernment movements. However, the 19 April incident in particular did have a considerable influence on Japanese students, among them the leaders of what was then the mainstream faction of the national students' union, Zengakuren.* Following that incident, on 26 April in Tokyo, 80,000 people took part in the "fifteenth united action movement" of the National Council for the Prevention of the Revision of the Security Treaty. Zengakuren too at this point organ-

---

*Federation of All-Japan Student Self-Governing Organizations prominent in political struggles in Japan, especially in the late 1950s.—Trans.

ized a rally of 5,500 students in front of the Diet, initiating a drive to burst through the gates into the grounds of the Diet building, thereby precipitating a major clash with the riot police. Twenty-eight people were reported injured. There is no denying that the action was influenced by the 19 April incident.

The 19 April incident was widely reported by the Japanese press, radio, and television. The violence of the clashes between students on the one hand and police and soldiers on the other was shocking. It was a time when the Japanese Security Treaty struggle had still to mature, and those who were participating in it watched the Korean situation with great concern. I can remember even now the tension with which we read the daily newspaper reports of the time. How painful it must have been for concerned Korean residents in Japan to watch the struggle by students in their homeland!

I was watching closely to see whether President Syngman Rhee would resign. At first, I thought it could not possibly come to be. On the other hand, I was concerned about how the United States would react. Finally, on 26 April—the very same day on which united action was taking place in Tokyo too—there was a huge demonstration in Seoul, and Syngman Rhee was forced to hand in his resignation. I was astonished at the achievement of the students, and at the same time shocked at the magnitude of the sacrifice they had paid. The Security Treaty struggles in Japan were bound to increase in intensity thereafter, and I remember wondering what I, as a university teacher, should say to my students.

Although, as I have suggested, the Korean April Revolution may have had some slight influence on the Security Treaty struggle in Japan, the two certainly cannot be said to have been closely connected. And so far as indirect links are concerned, the following two points should be raised.

First, in their relations with the United States, Japan and Korea, both anti-Communist countries, were placed in strategically similar positions. The Security Treaty struggle was initially a direct struggle against revision of the Japan-US Security Treaty. The aim of defending democracy was added after the railroading of the measure through the Lower House of the Diet on 19 May. The United States took the position that on no account would it accept the abandonment of the revision, and much less the repeal, of the Security Treaty.

At the same time, the US government persisted in the line that it could not yield on the question of maintaining its military and political position in Korea. So long as that condition was satisfied, there seems to have been no thought of giving unlimited support to the dictatorship of Syngman Rhee, which even in American eyes had gone too far. In any event, the United States had no plans to change its strategic position in the Far East in response to either the Security Treaty struggle or the April Revolution. Neither the Security Treaty struggle nor the April Revolution could break through that barrier. Through the medium of the two security treaties—one with Japan and the other with South Korea—the United States kept Japan and South Korea within its sphere of influence. In Japan, the Kishi cabinet resigned, but the revision of the Security Treaty was automatically accomplished. Korea's acting President Ho Chong, who took over from Syngman Rhee, sent the following telegram to Prime Minister Kishi on 27 June, acclaiming the new Japan-US Security Treaty: "It is my earnest hope that this Security Treaty will contribute much to further strengthening the position of the free world in the Far East in opposition to international Communist imperialism."

Thus, there is no denying that the shadow of the United States looms over both the April Revolution, with its successes and limitations, and the Security Treaty struggle, with its rise and then its collapse. I believe it is here that we should look for an indirect link between the April Revolution and the Security Treaty struggle.

The second point concerning indirect links is the question of the effect of these two events on subsequent relations between Japan and South Korea.

To begin with, subtle changes appeared in the Japan–South Korea relationship at the state level after the unrest of 1960. In Japan, the Ikeda cabinet switched the nation's course away from politics toward economics and launched the so-called income-doubling policy. In South Korea, too, there was a gradual change after 19 April from the Syngman Rhee government's anti-Communist, anti-Japanese political pose and its lackadaisical economic policy of relying largely on US aid. Anti-Communism was still strongly emphasized, but the anti-Japanese stance became merely a front, and a policy of rapprochement with Japan was begun, particularly in economic matters. This policy continued after the Park government took office in 1961. Rapprochement with Japan was pursued, and the course for the expansion of the Japanese economy into South Korea was charted. This course was confirmed in the basic treaty "normalizing" relations between Japan and South Korea in 1965. During these years, opposition to Japanese imperialism was played down in South Korea compared to the Syngman Rhee period, even in the field of education.

Thus the political agitation of 1960 gave way to economic growth, first in Japan, then in South Korea. In Japan, a broad strata of people with a "middle-class consciousness" emerged and were absorbed into the system. In South Korea too, a certain section of the people became involved in the Park government's policy of expanding the country's GNP. While the democratic forces critical of Park's dictatorship strengthened their base as a political force, it is undeniable that during the Park government's period of emphasis on economics, political apathy first began to spread. And in the twenty years since 1960 economic collusion between the highest authorities in Japan and South Korea has produced an almost inconceivable degree of corruption.

This "black relationship" between Japan and South Korea was not the only consequence of the upheavals of 1960. Out of them emerged too the seeds of a new solidarity and friendship between the thinking people of the two countries. Even though this did not develop sufficiently to become a real force, it came to exist on the level of consciousness and sensitivity. Both Japanese and Koreans, and in particular Japanese and Korean students, came to a mutual recognition in April, May, and June 1960 that there existed in the other country those who were fighting determinedly against an antidemocratic government in the one case and an autocratic military government in the other. They also gained a real sense of the existence of people on both sides of the sea opposed to the world strategy dictated by the United States and to American and Japanese neocolonialism.

In this way, however belatedly, people in Japan have become aware of the problem of discrimination against Koreans first during the years of Japanese imperialism and now in the years since the war against Korean residents in Japan. As part of this, movements have developed pressing for the release of political prisoners in South Korea, opposing the encroachments of the Japanese economy, the export of pollution to South Korea, and "*kisaeng*" tourism.* Furthermore, much scholarly work has been accomplished tracing Japan and Korea's ancient historical and cultural links. While not all of this is the result of the April Revolution and the Security Treaty struggle, nevertheless, since 1960, this positive sense of solidarity between the two peoples has grown.

These trends, both positive and negative, represent the sec-

---

*Often known also as "prostitution tourism," from the Korean work *kisaeng* (female entertainer). The *kisaeng* in traditional society was similar to the Japanese *geisha*. The word is now commonly used as a synonym for *prostitute*, while the term refers to the mass, all-male Japanese tour groups which, in the 1970s, headed first to South Korea and later to other countries in the region in quest of such companionship and drew widespread criticism both in Japan and elsewhere.—Trans.

ond set of indirect consequences of the 1960 disturbances.

II

Moving on from these considerations of relatedness, I find it highly interesting to compare the April Revolution and the Security Treaty struggle as historical phenomena.

There is no understating the importance of this subject. When students, ordinary working people, and intellectuals throw themselves into a political movement, particularly a popular movement of historical significance, we can clearly detect all those elements of cultural identity that have accumulated over the centuries. The Korean people's tradition of struggle against authority, originating in the Donghak peasant uprising of 1894 and the Samil independence movement of 1 March 1919, must have been reflected in the April Revolution, while the consciousness of peace garnered by the Japanese people from their experiences during the Second World War and the strength of popular movements since the war found expression in the Security Treaty struggle. In this way, the differences and similarities between Japan and South Korea in political, economic, and social structure, the nature of power, the character and strength of the people's movements, the internal contradictions which emerge as the movements develop: all of these are revealed. I believe such matters should be explored henceforth by both Japanese and Koreans as themes for comparative research.

I have neither the space nor the ability to develop such weighty themes in sufficient detail here. However, though it is a very limited approach, I would like to consider the differences and similarities in the character of the Security Treaty struggle and the April Revolution by examining one particular aspect and observing how that aspect was viewed by the people, and how, subsequently, it was absorbed into the tradition of the movement.

One hundred and ninety-one people were victims of the April

Revolution; one woman student lost her life in the Security Treaty struggle. To evaluate the two struggles by the number of victims is too simplistic; nor can we ignore the differences in the political situations of Japan and South Korea. However, when we consider that the casualties in the April Revolution in South Korea continued for a period of over forty days, from the heroic Masan uprising of 15 March to the 26 April incident when demonstrators in Seoul were fired upon, and that in terms of location it covered Seoul, Taegu, Pusan, Masan, Kongju, Chonju, Kwangju, Chongju, and Chunchon, we can understand how deep and how widespread was the resolve to overthrow the dictator President Syngman Rhee and to seek the restoration of democracy.

In contrast to this, once one victim had fallen in the 1960 Security Treaty struggle in Japan on 15 June, long-term continuation of the antigovernment struggle was seen as too difficult. It might also be said, of course, that it was not only impossible but also unnecessary. The midnight sit-in around the Diet on 18 June which followed a similar form of protest three nights earlier occupied the same position in Japan as the huge Seoul demonstration of 26 April, which came in the wake of the events of 19 April. However, at this time in Japan, the leaders of the Zengakuren student union federation, sensing the limits of their strength, did not attempt direct action, while the group of intellectuals with influence over the protest leaders feared that an explosion of violence might lead to the intervention of the Self-Defense Forces or to a sudden right-wing shift in the government, and they therefore worked hard to persuade the students and workers involved in the sit-in to refrain from acts of violence.

I feel that the difference between Seoul in April and Tokyo in June can to some extent be explained in terms of the fact that dictatorial power in Korea was incomparably stronger. Then again, the objectives of the Korean struggle against foreign influence, comprador mercantilism, feudalism, and dictatorship struck much more at the roots of the whole system than did the Japanese political objectives of opposition to the revision of the Japan-US Security Treaty and the defense of parliamentary democracy. Looking at it in retrospect, however, quite apart from the differences in the actual situation at the time, and the objectives of the struggles, we must also take into account the fact that Japan had no long historical tradition of popular struggle such as existed in Korea, with its Donghak peasant uprising and the Samil independence movement.

This point becomes so much clearer when we compare the way the struggle for democracy under the Park government has continued in Korea since 1960 with the way that the popular struggle in Japan has splintered. It would be a mistake to put the Park government and the Japanese Liberal Democratic Party government in the same category—there are too many differences in the degree of democratization. Nevertheless, I attach great importance to the fact that the unflagging struggles of Korean intellectuals, students, and workers are an extension of fighting power built up within the tradition of the Samil independence movement and the 19 April incident.

Thus the 19 April incident has been passed on and survives to the present day, but 15 June, unfortunately, has not survived because there was no tradition in which to incorporate it. The victims of 19 April have lived on for twenty years in the hearts of all those who have been engaged in the struggle for democracy in South Korea. Even President Park, who became sensitive to student moves whenever 19 April came round, was unable directly to criticize or denigrate the victims, and eventually he acknowledged the justice of their cause. Yet in Japan there are very few people who on 15 June remember and mourn for Kanba Michiko, the victim of the Security Treaty struggle.

Sometimes, when circumstances permit, on 15 June I meet up with some friends and pay a visit to the south service entrance of the Diet Building. We do no more than offer a bunch of flowers at the gate in silent prayer; but how many people know, I wonder, that the police try to put a stop even to that?

I find quite touching the similarities in content between a note left for her mother by Chin Yon Suk, a fourteen-year-old student killed by a bullet on 19 April, and Kanba Michiko's last words to her mother on 15 June.

Chin Yon Suk's farewell letter

It is getting late, mother, so I must leave without saying good-by. I'm going to fight to the last in this demonstration against the rigged election. All my friends—indeed all the students in the Republic of Korea—are shedding their blood for democracy in our country.

Mother, do not get angry with me for taking part in the demonstration. If we don't demonstrate, who will? I don't know much about life yet, but I do know the path the country and the people must take. Even now I can hear the shouts of the demonstrators.

I feel very restless. My school friends have all gone out prepared to die. I intend to offer my life in the struggle. Even if I should die during the demonstration, I will have no regrets. Mother, you will be very sad because you love me, but please rejoice for the future of our fellow countrymen and for the liberation of our people. My heart is already flying to the street.

I am in too much of a hurry—my hands refuse to move as fast as I want them to. Take good care of yourself. Let me say it again: I have made up my mind to offer my life. I have no time left, so I set my pen aside now. [Quoted from *Kankoku shigatsu kakumei* (The April Revolution in South Korea), Tokyo, Tsuge Shobō, 1977.]

Kanba Michiko, meanwhile, had the following conversation with her mother on the very day of the 15 June incident:

"Please don't join the demonstration. You're students! It isn't your business."

"Would it satisfy you if I alone didn't go? Should my friends go, and only I stay away?"

"I just cannot bear to see students demonstrating so fiercely and then staging sit-ins and getting hurt. . . . You can't expect to achieve anything unless the workers join forces with you and you act together."

"You're right. I know it's hopeless unless there's a general strike. But the workers have a living to make—it's hard for them. So the students will do it. Someone has to. Being arrested is certainly bad, but even that can't be helped. We must fight here! . . . Please, Mother, don't think it's enough for me to stay at home. There are vast numbers of housewives, but they're totally ineffectual because they're not organized." [Quoted from Kanba Toshio and Kanba Mitsuko, *Shi to kanashimi o koete* (Beyond Death and Sorrow), Tokyo, Yūkonsha, 1975.]

With these words, she left for the demonstration.

It is clear that both these students felt the same compulsion to take part in the demonstrations even though they expected the worst. However, it is what happened afterward that is different. Even now, surely many young people in South Korea know the name of Chin Yon Suk. Yet many Japanese students today have never heard of Kanba Michiko. Why the discrepancy?

Kanba Michiko was an activist in the mainstream faction of the federation of students' unions, Zengakuren. At this time there was a disagreement over tactics between Zengakuren, who advocated immediate and decisive action, and the National

Council for the Prevention of the Revision of the Security Treaty, which comprised in particular the General Council of Trade Unions (Sōhyō), the Japan Socialist Party, and the Japan Communist Party. When the students entered the Diet on that rainy night of 15 June, and Miss Kanba was killed in a clash with the police, the National Council joined in criticizing the police for going too far and in sincerely mourning her death. Not even the Communist Party, the sternest of Zengakuren's critics, censured it for her fate.

I see no difference between the death of Miss Kanba in the grounds of the Diet Building in June 1960 and that of Chin Yon Suk in Seoul. I also think it is wrong to stigmatize the Zengakuren students of that time as a "violent student mob."

After 15 June, the mass movement in Japan entered a period of schism, due in part to the difference over tactics at the time of the Security Treaty struggle. Since then, the Zengakuren has remained split. And, unfortunately, in the midst of these internecine arguments, the significance of Miss Kanba's death has been forgotten.

III

I have often heard it said by Koreans living in Japan that Koreans fuss over minor political differences and are politically immature. When I recall that in South Korea the tradition of the April Revolution lives on unchanged, I cannot help reflecting that it is the *Japanese* mass movement since 1960 which has been more obsessed with small differences. Why has this come about? It is something we as Japanese must think about.

I think inevitably of the line, "Oh raindrops, smash the rocks!" by Ham Sok Hon, which appeared in the journal *Sasanggye* (The World of Thought) in April 1961, one year after the April Revolution.

The venerable Ham Sok Hon, a Quaker, is even now, twenty years after 1960, a symbol to the Korean people of the movement for democracy. A year after Syngman Rhee's resignation in 1960, Ham spoke unequivocally of the failure of 19 April. The students fought well, he said, but the rats were not completely banished. What should be done? He called for another revolution.

What is a revolution? A revolution, he explained frankly, is an overturning. But it must have clear standards. "We call these standards truth and justice. The slogan of all reform and revolution must always be 'Return to truth and justice!' "

Thus a revolution is a principle of natural law rather than a stage in development. When authority is evil and repressive, overthrow it! What Ham had in mind was not the limited revolutions of recent centuries, the bourgeois or proletarian revolutions, for example, but the people's revolts against authority which have occurred on countless occasions right down from ancient times. Only in these is there any hope for the future.

A revolution, however, cannot be effected by student demonstrations alone, as was shown by 19 April. What is needed? A violent revolution? No, Ham Sok Hon looks to a revolution brought about through an awakening and rousing of the people. Awaken the people's anger! There are two causes for that anger. One is hunger. The other is injustice. Ham stresses the righteous anger of those suffering injustice.

He speaks of his boundless trust in the masses. While intellectuals too are indispensable to revolution, they "have the drawback of always tending to float upwards like balloons." It is therefore important to awaken the masses. "Teach the people!" he says.

> Treat them as human beings! Entrust them with important business! Stop thinking conceitedly, "We'll do it!" The one who does things is God, and the people are His representatives. Tell them, "The affairs

of the nation rest in your hands. The fate of the world depends upon you!'' And dissolve yourself into the people just as salt dissolves naturally in water.

The role of students? They are the people's activists; they must become raindrops beating upon the masses. Even if the hearts of the people were of rock, ''if they hammer away ceaselessly at it, the rock will crumble in the end.'' But the people are far from being rock—they are the roots, the seeds. When Ham Sok Hon refers to the people, he does not mean just the working class. He means farmers, workers, ordinary people, housewives, young people, students, the unemployed, and the lumpen proletariat. His is a theory of the people rather than of a class.

There is one more important point he makes. He attaches great importance to the social system and is consequently in favor of a revolution in the system. This is because people are shaped by the framework of society. Put the other way round, he believes that people can change, and he believes in the possibility of salvation, and it is this which forms the basis for breaking the vicious circle of social and political vengeance.

Have the people in South Korea come to follow the ideas of Ham Sok Hon or his Catholic colleague Kim Chi Ha only because under the autocratic South Korean government they do not have the freedom to support Marxism? I do not think so. These great men are confidently spreading a modern theory of revolution from an ideological position different from that of Marxism, one which, however, does not totally repudiate Marxism.

Ham calls for love rather than violence. Can we simply pigeonhole such a theory of revolution as juvenile? On the contrary, that idea has continued to sustain the solidarity of the Korean people at least for the past twenty years without leading the struggle for democracy into fragmentation and dispersal. Indeed, as an idea it can be traced even further back, to the tenacity and solidarity of the resistance movement of the Korean people under the rule of Japanese imperialism.

I do not simply deny Marxism. It is a fact that many revolutions have taken place under its guidance, particularly in the developing areas of the world. I have the impression, however, that while Marxism is useful as a weapon to bring about revolution, it is not so useful as a weapon for the construction of a new society. Its biggest problem is that it is seen to repress human rights in various ways. I wonder why this is.

Let me conclude my discussion of these points here. As a final word, however, it cannot be denied that the movement against authority in Japan broke up after 1960. Under those circumstances, has the idea of solidarity in its true sense been born in Japan? Are there now in Japan active intellectuals on a par with Ham Sok Hon or Kim Chi Ha, who continue to appeal not just for the unification of the north and south of their country but also for solidarity in the movement for democracy? We Japanese need to think and reflect deeply on these matters.

▌▌▌ Chapter Eight ▌▌▌

Thoughts from Minamata

I know it is both odd and presumptuous that I have elected to deliver "Thoughts from Minamata." Of course, the citizens of Minamata are always thinking, questioning, and expressing opinions "from Minamata," and it is they naturally who are qualified to do so. In contrast, we observers from Tokyo or from Kyoto only visit Minamata, reflect on it, and return again to Tokyo or to Kyoto. However, it is my contention that there ought to be a way of seeing and thinking about Minamata from Minamata, and of seeing Tokyo, Japan, Asia, or the whole world from the viewpoint of Minamata. Needless to say, this is how the people of Minamata see things. We as outsiders must imbibe deeply of this vision from them, so that little by little it becomes our own.

Let me add, however, that while we outsiders must realize that we cannot completely identify with the "from Minamata" view of the people of Minamata, it is not necessarily true to state that everyone in Minamata sees things honestly "from Minamata." Thus it is so important for all of us, not only outsiders

NOTE: This chapter was originally delivered as a talk in Minamata in August of 1977 under the auspices of the Minamata Disease Center and the publishing house Sōshisha. The introductory paragraph has been deleted, and some minor revisions have been made. See also footnote on page 111.

but also people living in Minamata, to think "from Minamata."

It should be obvious that this "from Minamata" is something
both concrete and general, real and symbolic. It means that each
and every one of us should look at Japan from the standpoint
of our own region, our own locality. It is only when we have
our feet securely planted in local soil that Japan and, just possibly, Asia becomes visible. I submit that our fundamental
problem today is that each of us, or all of us collectively as a
nation, has long lost this vantage point.

But to think "from Minamata" does not just mean to think
"from Minamata disease." It means thinking about the entirety
of the Minamata region and its history, how man has lived here
from the time that fishing people first settled in the area, or along
the coast of the Shiranui Sea; in other words, history from
prehistoric times down to the present, through ancient, medieval,
and feudal times and through the Meiji Restoration. Not that
I have the space or the qualifications to do so here and now,
but I feel it is important to think "from Minamata" in the way
I have suggested.

Let's look at some milestones in the long history of Minamata.
It was in 1908 that the Chisso Corporation, then the Japan
Nitrogen Company, established a plant in Minamata. How
was the Minamata community affected? Much later, on 15 August 1945, Japan met its disastrous defeat in the Second World
War—the most momentous event for the country since the Meiji
Restoration of 1868. It must have also been an event of
magnitude for Minamata. How did the people of Minamata
feel about it? What did they have to say about it among
themselves? How did they react? Then, in 1953 or thereabouts,
cats began to go mad and die. At the same time, people suddenly began to show strange symptoms, and by 1956 many people had contracted this shocking "mystery disease." Since then
almost thirty years have passed—long enough for us to think
in historical terms. Considering the time span and the scope

of the problem, there is a great deal that calls for long, earnest, and many-sided reflection.

In 1945, the year of Japan's defeat, I was twenty-eight years old. On that day, at exactly twelve noon, I was listening in Yasuda Hall at the University of Tokyo to the broadcast of the imperial proclamation "ending" the war.

Fukuzawa Yukichi* once said that he had lived "two lives in one." What he meant was that his life had spanned two distinctly different periods, before and after the Meiji Restoration of 1868. In a way I too have lived "two lives in one." Until the age of twenty-eight I experienced the age of prewar and wartime militarism, and since then have experienced thirty and more years of postwar Japan.

For quite a long time prior to August 1945, I was expecting Japan's defeat in war. That forecast proved to be correct, but my forecast for postwar Japan was wide of the mark. Bluntly speaking, I am not at all pleased with what I see of Japan as it is today. The postwar Japan I had anticipated was rather different. Of late, I feel tempted to try to understand why I was correct in predicting defeat but not in predicting the nature of postwar Japan.

In this regard one thing strikes me above all others. That is that we have all been bombarded with the notion—through every medium, be it school textbooks, newspapers, or television—that the militarist age came to an end as of 15 August 1945 and that then an entirely new age, one of democracy, dawned in Japan. This notion would be accepted by an overwhelming majority; it is part of a national consensus.

I do not deny that 15 August 1945 marked the end of a chapter in Japanese history, but I have long thought that it is contrary to the evidence to think that there was as a result a qualitative change in every aspect of life in Japan. How are we to interpret

---

*1835–1901. Prominent philosopher of liberal enlightenment thinking in the years following Japan's opening to Western influence in the mid-nineteenth century.—Trans.

the continuities and the discontinuities of Japan before and after 1945?

As good a way as any to ascertain what defeat in war meant to Japan is to read Japanese newspapers carefully day by day for the period before and after 15 August 1945. Nor is there any great difficulty involved in this, as most public libraries to-day have bound, reduced-size copies of the newspapers. The actual nature of the defeat thereby becomes clear. The peculiar thing you realize is that in the period spanning the time of defeat in the war the tone of the Japanese press does not change at all. Indeed it is amazing how the tone remains the same. Day after day, on 14 August, on 15, 16, and 17 August, what was stressed was that Japan was ruled by an emperor of a lineal suc-- cession unbroken for ages eternal, and that we the Japanese would protect this national polity to the bitter end. Not a word was written about democracy at that stage; only gradually did the tone of press commentaries begin to change. At the time of the defeat, the Higashikuni cabinet was formed, and Prince Higashikuni tentatively began to use the word "democracy," but he also said democracy meant the Five Article Charter Oath, of the first year of Meiji, 1868. In short, it was continuity rather than radical change that marked the history of Japan through defeat in war on 15 August. This, one need hardly add, was not unrelated to the fact that the defeat was brought about by external forces alone.

There is, of course, no denying that significant changes oc- curred, especially involving the promulgation of the new con- stitution in 1946. However, at the same time, the forces that survived intact from prewar Japan were considerable. The monarch became a symbol, but Japan remained a monarchy. Most important, Japanese capitalism survived; there were moves to dissolve the *zaibatsu*,* but in no time at all this policy was

---

*The large prewar financial and industrial organizations based on ownership and control by family trusts.—Trans.

emasculated. In defeated Germany and Italy, newspapers which had collaborated with the Nazi and Fascist regimes were all abolished, and the proprietors tried as war criminals. In Japan, by contrast, there was some measure of democratization within the press, but all the major nationwide newspapers—such as the *Asahi, Mainichi,* and *Yomiuri*—remained intact, together with their titles. The ideas of those in power did not change, and it proved extremely difficult for the consciousness of the people to free itself from the shackles of the old system.

The situation in Minamata can have been little different. With the defeat, there were some purges of old military and political leaders as well as of some leading businessmen. There were moves to dissolve the *zaibatsu,* but apart from the dismissal of a few top executives, the so-called new *zaibatsu,* which included Chisso Corporation, were not seriously affected. So Chisso survived the defeat intact. Chisso had started production in 1908, then expanded into Korea in 1927 with the establishment of a huge plant at Hungnam. After the war, the company had to give up the plant in Korea altogether. The Minamata factory sustained serious damage from air raids during the war, but it was reopened and continues to operate today. Thus, Minamata has been Chisso's company town without change through the prewar, wartime, and postwar eras.

The first signs of the Minamata disease problem were apparent from around 1953 with reduced fish catches, cats going mad and dying, and so on. Pollution of the sea was nothing new; it had already been evident before the war, and Minamata fishermen had many times negotiated with Chisso about the matter.

In 1949, the town of Minamata became a city. Its population at the time was 42,000. Today, the city has a population of 36,000. This is very much a characteristic of postwar Japan; small cities such as Minamata have not gained in population since the end of the war; rather they have declined. Minamata saw a slight and temporary increase, but of late it has continued to decline slowly. Although this decline is not unrelated to the contraction in the scale of Chisso, neither phenomenon has been particularly dramatic. Tokyo at the end of the war had a population of 1.9 million people; now it has 11 million, a fivefold increase. The contrast between Minamata and Tokyo is indicative of population trends in postwar Japan.

From 1949 on, there was a drastic decline in the fish catch from Minamata Bay—in the catch of prawns, sardines, octopuses, bream, and other varieties. The average annual catch between 1950 and 1953 was about 460 tons. It declined to 280 tons in 1954, 172 tons in 1955, and a mere 96 tons in 1956—nearly an 80-percent reduction in just three years!

This dramatic decline in the fish catch exactly parallels the rapid expansion in output from the Chisso plant at the time. A cursory survey of Japan's postwar economic history shows that it was in 1955, or some ten years after the end of the war, that industrial production nationwide recovered to the level of 1935. In the case of Minamata, the population did not increase significantly but Chisso's production climbed rapidly. Some examples will illustrate the point. Take vinyl chloride, for instance. At the outset, production was low—monthly output in 1951 was 150 tons. This rose to 250 tons in 1953, 340 tons in 1954, and then a rapid rise to 1,500 tons in 1957. During this period, mercury pollution continued to escalate. Growth rates were greater in the chemical sector of the economy than in any other. This is the context in which Minamata disease broke out.

Chisso, chasing after profits like any other business corporation, pursued a policy of rapid expansion almost as soon as the war ended. The company has always been characterized by its lack of concern for the safety of workers. Chisso was part of the so-called Noguchi new *zaibatsu*. Noguchi Shitagau, its founder, was obviously an outstanding person. However, because it had to compete against larger, older-established *zaibatsu* firms, Chisso was inclined to cut corners and go all out to increase production. This led to many disasters from prewar times on. There were disastrous explosions in 1927, 1928, 1930, 1934, and 1937, resulting each time in extensive casualties among the workers.

A man who used to work in the factory around 1935 has testified that, when he applied for the job, he was addressed in the following terms by the company's personnel department at an interview: "The work in the factory is extremely dangerous. You may be blown up and killed. Do you still want the job?" To this extent was safety ignored. After the war the same system continued. In 1951, the company's industrial casualty rate amounted to an astonishing 422 out of 1,000 workers. This figure may include minor injuries, but even so the factory was so dangerous that within the space of one year almost half the entire work force encountered injury of one kind or another. The attitude of this enterprise to its workers was the same after 15 August as it was before.

Recently people have come to think that the Minamata issue is a thing of the past. The citizens of Minamata know full well that this is not the case. Our most important task remains that of broadcasting the reality of the suffering. The people of Minamata face a dilemma: they would like to forget the Minamata disease and are fed up with thinking about it, but at the same time they would also like everyone in Japan to know the true horror of the suffering wrought by Minamata disease. What is the reality of this suffering?

Minamata disease arises when physical problems occur due to mercury poisoning; in other words, it is a health question. But I doubt very much if the reality of the harm caused by Minamata disease can be grasped on a purely medical basis. It commences on a medical level and then spreads to the psychological and social levels. The problem of how to cope with and provide relief for the harm done on the nonmedical level has yet to be considered.

Even on the purely medical level, serious new problems continue to appear. Recently, for example, Professor Harada Masazumi of Kumamoto University, during the course of independent medical examinations, discovered an additional seven children who could definitely be designated as congenitally diseased and a further twenty-one cases of children whose condition appeared to be related to Minamata disease even though the classical symptoms of Minamata disease had not appeared. I believe this points to the need to expand greatly the concept of Minamata disease.

Until now, Minamata disease has been diagnosed in accordance with, or on the basis of, the so-called Hunter-Russell syndrome. In medical terminology there are various difficult expressions for the narrowing of the visual field, hardness of hearing, motor malfunction; in other words, symptoms affecting the eyes, ears, mouth, hands, and feet. The eye's field of vision shrinks, the ear's auditory capacity decreases, the mouth becomes unable to utter sounds distinctly, the hands lose their sensation and tremble, and the legs tend to swell so that it becomes impossible to walk properly. In extreme cases, the brain is completely affected and total body convulsions occur.

However, our understanding of Minamata disease does not end there. For example, from 1960 to 1965 the problem of congenitally affected children became a serious issue, and again now attention is focused on how better to define the manner in which the disease appears in its congenital form. It is this, I believe, which Professor Harada wants to emphasize. We are gradually coming to understand that children so far diagnosed as congenital victims of Minamata disease represent only a very small segment of the actual extent of damage.

I think we can consider congenital cases in the following five categories, bearing in mind that congenital victims of Minamata disease who were born and grew up survived only because of the strength of the life force within them. Those who were miscarried at the foetal stage form the first category. The second category is comprised of children who were stillborn. Category three includes all those children so far generally recognized as congenital victims of Minamata disease. Category four includes those children who display only some of the classic symptoms. Finally, in the fifth category are those children whom the law does not acknowledge as congenital cases of Minamata disease but who have complaints of various kinds, physical or mental. These complaints include various symptoms such as low resistance to fatigue, headaches, stiff shoulders, lack of stamina both physical and mental, and also liver disorders. They are unable to keep up with other children in their school work. All of these children come either from areas where many victims have been identified or from families in which either parents or brothers or sisters have been designated as sufferers, or have applied for such designation. I believe that most of those in this last category are actually congenital Minamata disease sufferers.

The physical and mental disorders of the children are sometimes completely medical in character; in these cases, the damage is directly attributable to Minamata disease. But some are likely to be psychologically based. Take the case of a child complaining of some psychologically based physical or mental disorder whose family includes a number of victims of the disease and whose family life is being disrupted because no one in the family can work. In this sort of case, whether or not the family receives compensation and can make ends meet as a result, it must be said that the main cause of the child's psychological ailment is that the parents are victims of Minamata disease. This child's case should be recognized as Minamata disease, as part of the Minamata reality, even when it is psychologically based. The suffering caused by Minamata disease is not confined to the medical dimension but includes also psychologically based physical and mental disorders. We can expect that children so affected will face problems in the future over employment or marriage even though they may not be recognized as sufferers or congenital victims of Minamata disease. Such social problems, in the final analysis, must be recognized as being caused by Minamata disease. Likewise, various emotional strains and problems may develop because village industry collapses, or the fishing business no longer pays, or else human relations within the village suffer as some are awarded compensation, some are still applying, and others have been rejected. The village as the place which sustains the livelihood of the community is destroyed. All these destructive phenomena must be seen as suffering caused by Minamata disease. In brief, when we talk of relief for Minamata victims or of the reality of their suffering, we must expand the scope of the discussion to include all the above-mentioned dimensions.

Relief itself must not consist solely of payment of compensation to sufferers. But what apart from money are Chisso and the government contemplating? And what ideas do they have for eliminating social prejudice against victims of Minamata disease and their families? It is absolutely unforgivable they should simply fold their arms and do nothing or call those who are applying for compensation "money mad."

I would like next to consider something which is already a problem and likely to become an ever greater one: the question of the second-generation Minamata disease victims, the children born to parents who suffer from the disease.

People often say that no babies congenitally affected by Minamata disease have been born since around 1960. However, the youngest actually recognized congenital Minamata disease patient as of 1977 was fourteen years old, that is to say, he was born three years after 1960. We cannot even be sure that there are no younger victims. Minamata disease takes two forms: direct mercury poisoning resulting from the intake of seafood, and congenital affliction resulting from prenatal absorption of mercury through the mother's placenta. Each form in turn may be either acute or chronic. Acute cases occurred in particular between approximately 1953 and 1960. And although congenital cases are said not to have occurred from about 1960, there is continuing evidence of their persistence in chronic form. The appearance of the disease in chronic form, therefore, is what

is important. Both chronic Minamata disease and chronic congenital Minamata disease can appear among children. Logic
suggests that this should be so, but in addition the investigations of Professor Harada and others have borne this out.

The business of diagnosing whether a child has Minamata
disease should not be taken lightly; the child's future happiness
is at stake. Extreme caution must be exercised, but at the same
time it must be remembered that the child's future may be
jeopardized if he or she actually has the disease. How can these
dangers best be brushed aside or overcome? In my view, the
first step is to recognize the truth as the truth, to do so from
both a scientific and a human standpoint, rather than to conceal the truth or flee from it.

For over ten years now, we have been facing the problem
of the "second-generation atomic-bomb victims." Children were
born to parents who had been exposed to radiation at Hiroshima;
they grew up, and now are at universities or of marriageable
age. There are some among the second-generation atomic-bomb
victims who despite a surface appearance of good health are conscious of various troubles. And even those who are not conscious
of any physical problem encounter various handicaps, simply
because they are children of atomic-bomb victims. I once held
a seminar at my college on the subject of Minamata disease.
One of the students who took part was a young woman from
Hiroshima; at the time of the explosion, her mother had been
pregnant with her older sister. When her sister was considering marriage, the prospective husband's family objected, saying that she had been a child in the womb when the atomic bomb
fell. My student then became conscious of the problem for the
first time, and became very anxious about her own future—
about marriage and having children. When she came to see me,
I had this to say to her:

> There is no need for you to be afraid. When you are
> going to marry, if your partner is truly a man of

understanding and trust, you should tell him the truth and assure him that there is little to worry about concerning your health or that of your future children. If, on the other hand, you are not sure he would understand, I don't believe you need to tell him the whole truth at that stage.

But there is always some possibility, however slight, of misfortune. Medically speaking too, there can be no absolute certainty, so I reminded my student that in any case one out of thirty children born to perfectly healthy parents turns out to be handicapped in one way or another. If everyone were afraid of such a possibility, no one would have children. The fact of her mother having been exposed to the atomic blast may have had a slightly adverse effect on the balance of possibilities, but the odds were of the same general order in her case as in the case of those whose parents were quite normal. Still, suppose a handicapped child were born, what then? Divorce on such grounds is almost unknown. It is far more common for the parents to pitch in together and help each other out in rearing the child. Of course it is important to build a system which, individually and socially, supports such parents; but the parents of a handicapped child, as parents, simply have to accept the responsibility and to cope with it to the best of their ability.

What I said to this student was based on my own personal experience. I had a severely handicapped younger brother; he died at the age of sixteen. Once I visited Meisuien, the home for Minamata disease patients. One of the patients was a severely mentally and physically handicapped young man, who sucked and bit his fingers, slapped his own face, waved his hands about in front of his eyes, and so on. He was quite unable to feed himself.

I was completely taken aback when I first saw him; he was the living image of my dead brother. The resemblance was astonishing. The cause of my brother's affliction was never known. A thorough examination was conducted in Kyushu University Hospital in, I think, 1926, but it was fruitless. No one without actual experience can understand how much the whole family of such a child suffers. Even as a grown youth, diapers were indispensable for my brother; and then he had to be fed at mealtime. Truly those were days filled with desperate suffering. Later, after his death, my mother confessed that many times she had thought to herself that she could not die leaving this son to survive her. I suppose such feelings must be very common among mothers and fathers in such a position, and yet they seem to me to be of quite extraordinary pathos. "Poor child" was my mother's habitual phrase. Looking back, I can think of no better words with which to express one's feelings toward a child born with such an affliction.

Every day was a day of desperate struggle with life itself, without a moment's rest for the spirit. And it was a struggle in which there was no hope; although at the same time we could never quite abandon the hope that some day there might be some improvement. My parents suffered from the time he was born until the time when, at the age of sixteen, he died.

But if in their hearts 99.9 percent was despair, there was also that 0.1 percent of hope. At that time, there was no institution for the permanent care of handicapped children. Anyway my parents wanted to look after him themselves. This is the sort of thing it means to be a "poor child." Thus did my mother live torn between despair of life and hope for life, and when I recall how heavy were the odds against her hope, I cannot help but feel, "Poor mother—."

What my mother tried hardest to do was to teach my brother to say when he needed to go to the toilet. The sight of a grown teenage boy, still in diapers and yet constantly wetting the *tatami* floor, was enough to make one want to weep. So my mother tried so hard. But with what results? Perhaps he would make an effort to tell us about half the time. He was healthy enough physically to walk up to others in the family and make some sign by hand. You may laugh if I say that this amounted to education for my brother—but what a relief it was for the family that one time in two he did not wet himself. For our family, that the boy should be able to go to the toilet even fifty percent of the time was of far, far greater moment than that he should learn differential and integral calculus or a bit of English. Perhaps it was this belief in the potentiality of life—however slight—that sustained my mother in the task of teaching my brother.

Setting eyes on the congenitally afflicted children of Minamata, most people fall prey to a deep feeling of despair. The youth in the Meisuien home who so resembles my dead brother is now over twenty. He can do nothing, he comprehends nothing. Yet the people who look after him and his frequent visitors will tell you that he is not without feeling. My brother too had feelings, which he expressed in various ways. When he was happy, he smiled; on other occasions he looked as if he was about to say something or to ask a question. The children of Meisuien are like this too. They have the same expressions.

Some young people who are congenital victims of Minamata disease continue to live at home. One such young man I met spoke to me, and, despite great difficulties making sense of his words, I could more or less understand. When he walked, he walked like a child with infantile paralysis. Although we only talked for thirty or forty minutes, I came to think that his intellect was quite developed and that he was astonishingly rich in emotion. It was he, I believe, who had appeared when he was younger in the film *Minamata Disease: The Medical Story.* Professor Harada had this to say about the boy: "Although this child's face suggests a firm and serious character, his intelligence has not developed beyond the age of about four or five." This comment was made seven or eight years ago. My impression is that he seems to have developed considerably since then. Or maybe even then, in some senses, he was more intelligent than a four or five year old. According to Professor Harada, some congenital sufferers did in fact develop rapidly intellectually and psychologically whenever they had the chance to participate in something, whether it be court proceedings or a social movement.

Such potential may exist in any individual. How can this potential be developed? Once one is rejected as hopeless, that potential is destroyed. If there are people who will dedicate themselves to helping, then the potential will be realized. Moreover, there will be no growth if there is absolutely no contact with the outside world or if the child remains cooped up at home. It is when friends and helpers stimulate him or her that the patient changes, however slightly.

The existence of this potential is one reality. On the other hand, however, there are cases which are all but hopeless. Indeed, when you consider that Minamata disease has been pronounced medically incurable, it is hopeless. Nevertheless, the desire and the will to live as a human being exists, so we must try to develop this potential. We cannot simply give up hope. Yet we would be deluding ourselves if we thought there was a hundred-percent chance of success. The question is what we can do, what room we have for action between the poles of despair and hope?

This, I believe, should be our basic attitude toward Minamata disease, congenital or otherwise. At the same time, this raises one of the most fundamental problems in contemporary Japanese education.

Allow me to digress a moment about one aspect of what I experience as a teacher. I believe this experience is both particular and universal. In Japanese education today, the gaps between schools have reached an alarming level. On the high school level, regular high schools are considered superior to vocational high schools. In higher education, there are hierarchical gaps between "first rate," "second rate," and "third rate" universities. Four-year and two-year institutions are seen not just as different types of education, but as superior versus inferior. The unequivocal rule for determining quality is the degree of difficulty of the entrance examination, and this may be indicated by a refined system of grading points according to "deviation from standards." The criterion of scholastic ability determines everything.

Yet, it should be obvious that anyone who does not recognize that scholastic ability is only a small component of a person's worth is not qualified to discuss contemporary education. It is high time in my opinion that we realized that education cannot be considered in these terms alone. Yet only a very few of today's teachers have adopted this view, and very rare is the student who does not feel disadvantaged if he lacks scholastic ability. Students in recent years have given me a very strong impression of docility, to the point where at times they even appear quite cowed in spirit. This seems to be a phenomenon found throughout Japan.

We hear, it is true, of some students—mainly junior-high and high school students—who commit acts of violence against their teachers and friends. They are, however, only a small minority, while the majority today seem dispirited and passive. I think the latter phenomenon is the more serious of the two. Ask them in a classroom to read aloud from a textbook, and they read only in a faint and feeble voice. Ask them for their opinion, and they scarcely respond at all. In the past, students who took part in the Composition from Life Movement produced a host of fascinating essays. Not anymore.

This seems to be the case in schools throughout Japan. Why do the students cower so? Is it that children today are gutless? Is it because teachers today are no good? Certainly I believe we teachers cannot evade responsibility, but Japanese education as a whole is becoming so distorted that it is no longer worthy of the name "education."

Students have at all levels become passive, or rather, been reduced to passivity, and *that* I feel is the root cause of the destruction of education.

In 1971, the Central Council for Education submitted an important report to the Ministry of Education on the direction that Japanese education should take. The most frequently used words in the report are "competence" and "aptitude." Such words may be understood in various ways, but what they mean in practice is that a given level of "competence" is necessary before one can qualify for university entrance or for a particular job, and by extension that some individuals are suited to manual labor and others are fit for mental work. Both competence and aptitude are objective yardsticks applied to young people from without; they are useless in the evaluation of the character which the individual develops for himself from within. Students tend to conform to a mold designed from without, or they make a target of this mold and work feverishly toward it. School education has become nothing more than a tool in this process.

The result, inevitably, is that many "fall by the wayside." Just imagine what impact the label of failure through high school and at university has on the formation of a person's character. Imagine being continually humiliated in this way throughout one's childhood and youth.

I believe education cannot be reconstituted unless we make a fresh start by replacing the externally imposed standards of "competence" and "aptitude" with the "aspiration" and "potential" of the individual child. At all universities without exception, students have become docile. A passive meekness is pervasive. Children, high-spirited in primary school, have the buds of independence and autonomy nipped by the time they finish high school. I want somehow to challenge them so they break out of their mold. That is how I see my task as a teacher. Everything is determined by whether the students themselves aspire from within.

If education is understood as a process of the fostering of growth in each individual, then education of congenitally afflicted children, though it may seem a very special case, is actually not in substance different.

Take as an example the case of congenital patients who gradually developed a keen sense of judgement in the course of attending the Minamata court hearings. We can make similar observations about many other young patients and second-generation sufferers. In the Meisuien home there is a congenital patient, a girl whom I will call K. She can talk, and is mentally quite developed. She has, in addition, a special talent: she can understand what other severely handicapped patients are saying. In that sense her "competence" is far greater than ours. And little K enjoys the trust of all the staff members of the home.

She works hard there. Mind you, she is a patient, but she works like a staff member. When other patients want to sit out to sunbathe, she helps them move or carries their blankets. Since she started to be involved in such work, she has made considerable improvement in her own development. I believe the same process has occurred with other patients.

If, instead, you place a patient in an institution and isolate him or her from the outside world, that patient will tend to lose interest, and things will degenerate. How can the potential in such children be brought out? I think the secret is to awaken the child's desire for activity, and in the case of the congenital Minamata patients this requires in turn that those around the children possess a strong faith in the latent ability of each one of them. It is not educational activities in school which most stimulate growth or self-realization on the part of congenital patients but participation in society and communication with other patients in small-group activity. This is of great significance.

There is one other factor we must not forget when considering the problems of daily living and education for second-generation sufferers and young patients generally, and that is work—the problem of a vocation. It is not only that people need to work in order to make a living. Work is an extremely important function for every man and woman regardless of whether their lives are already financially assured. Recognized sufferers from Minamata disease receive either compensation or a pension, and they may be free from the financial need to work. Even so, it is important for them to work, to have a vocation.

I have heard, and I well understand, that there are various opinions on the question of compensation, even in Minamata. Although it may be a simplistic comparison, consider the case of a person injured in a road accident who becomes unable to work for the rest of his or her life. How much compensation would such a person be likely to receive? The payment would be a good deal more than the amount paid to Minamata victims. But would anyone say it was excessive?

Even when compensation awards are made, the problem of a vocation remains. One adult Minamata disease patient who is still capable of some work went to consult with a member of the local council. "You are getting compensation as well as a pension," he was told. "You can live without working. There is no need for you to work." This is utterly wrong-headed. It is work that makes life worth living. A farmer sows seeds. A fisherman fishes. In so many different ways, people simply want to work. It is clear beyond any possible obfuscation that the real relief for Minamata patients is to provide those who want to work with somewhere to do that work.

This leads us on to other problems. Consider the case of K, the girl who helps other patients and interprets for them at the Meisuien home. She works. The worst-stricken patients receive a pension of ¥80,000 a month. K is getting a pension of a little over ¥50,000 a month. At the same time she receives an allowance of ¥3,000 per month from the Meisuien home in recognition of the work she does. And a good thing she does too; a person should be paid for his or her labor. But suppose she was not receiving a pension, or that she was receiving one but it was being put in trust for her. Then her attitude toward her work would change; she would see herself as being paid no more than ¥3,000 per month even though she worked as hard as she could while others were paid more—perhaps ¥50,000, ¥60,000, or ¥100,000.

If I may be forgiven for taking my own workplace as an example again, the college where I teach has a system of equal pay for all staff, teaching and clerical. Differentials result from age only. So a clerk who started work after leaving high school and an assistant professor with a thesis behind him receive exactly the same salary and bonuses if they are of the same age. This is a highly unusual system, and I imagine there are very few places in Japan—be they business corporations, schools, or government offices—which have anything resembling it.

This sort of system is not without its problems. For instance, some might say that the investment in time and money in studying for four years at a university is meaningless if in the end the salary is the same as that of a high-school graduate. But when you think about it, it might be argued that being able to go to a university—and thereby study that much more, or play that much more—is worthwhile in itself. Could it not be seen as its own reward? Compare this system with the pay structure to be found in most universities and colleges. Normally teaching staff are divided into ranks—lecturer, assistant professor, and professor among them—each with a different pay scale. Even within the rank of professor, there are differences in pay scale depending on whether or not the professor in question teaches in graduate school. The differentials are finely calculated. What is the philosophical basis for such an artificial system of detailed differentials?

All schools have teachers, clerks, and general staff. What does this signify? There is mental work, clerical work, and physical work, and each is of a different class and each involves a different pay scale. Many have argued that such a division of labor is wrong. They say that in a future utopia a person may be at once politician, artist, baker, farmer, and fisherman. It takes little reflection to conclude that such a situation would be much healthier.

The accepted principle behind remuneration is that payment varies according to ability. But what is normally referred to as ability is often so much humbug. The board of education appoints one person headmaster and another person deputy headmaster believing that each appointee has the abilities appropriate to the respective position. However, sociologically speaking, it is often more accurate to say that it is because one has become head of a department or organization that one is able to demonstrate one's ability rather than to say that the promotion itself is attributable to the ability.

So the principle behind the elaborately differentiated pay system is remuneration according to ability. This principle is also accepted under a socialist system. But if a different standard is applied, an entirely different result emerges. Where A is able to do 80 and B is able to do only 60, according to the above principle it is considered fair to pay A ¥80,000 and B ¥60,000. But presuming that both expounded equal amounts of effort and both did their best, would it not be fair for them to receive *equal* pay, either ¥80,000 or ¥60,000? No one can argue that the first system is superior to the second. They are based on different principles.

A few days ago, two members of the staff from the Minamata Disease Center and a young patient came to my house in Kyoto and stayed overnight. They were transporting tangerine oranges by truck to Nagano and returning with a load of Nagano apples. As Kyoto is midway between Kyushu and Nagano, they stayed at my house overnight. It was the first time the young Minamata patient had traveled so far from home. That made him happy. He was working. Physically he is weak, so thin that he has almost no shoulder muscles. The loading and unloading of heavy cartons of oranges and apples is beyond him. Nevertheless he works hard in his own way. How then to pay the three of them? Who would argue if they received the same amount? No one in the Center—either staff or patients—complains of inequality. These values are not beyond our reach.

Not that I imagine, even in my wildest dreams, that Japan could change in this way overnight. And yet, change it should,

I believe. The point at issue here is what the patient's labor involves and by what standard it should be evaluated. A business corporation would say that it could not afford to employ a disabled person who could do only thirty percent of what a healthy person could do; if they did employ him, they would probably pay him only thirty percent of what a healthy employee would receive. This is logical from the business point of view. What would we say, however, if K, the congenital patient at the Meisuien home, were to say she no longer wanted her ¥3,000 but instead preferred to receive a monthly salary of say ¥60,000 or ¥80,000, that if she received a salary of this order she would not need a pension until she was no longer able to work?

Even within Minamata, I understand there is some whispering behind patients' backs that applicants for compensation and pensions are simply money mad. To my way of thinking, compensation and pensions are but an expedient under current social conditions where the communal system of mutual help has vanished and an egalitarian system of remuneration not based on ability has yet to come into existence. Critics of compensation, if serious about their criticism, should be prepared to adopt patients themselves. They should take full responsibility for the personal welfare of congenital Minamata disease victims; they should take care of them in their daily life and help to find them jobs. If there were people—whether relatives, friends, neighbors, or members of the community—prepared to make this commitment and act upon it, neither compensation nor pensions would be necessary. But are there people willing to undertake such a task?

There was a time when each community used to have some sort of mutual aid system, however flawed. But that time has long since disappeared. At some point in the future, what we now consider utopian may come to be; but that is for the future. Under present circumstances, where the social structure is anything but utopian, it is only right that the victims demand compensation and pensions. It is possible that as a result there may be some degeneration, tangible or intangible, mental or physical, among some patients. But if they are to be criticized for being money mad, let us first recognize that the root of the evil lies in the extraordinary money mania that grips the whole country. Let there be an end to criticism of hard-won compensation and pensions voiced by those who would slander rather than help and by a society which denies work to young patients who have the will to work.

Minamata disease patients and their children must not be deprived of the joy of work, of an occupation that gives meaning to life. However, it appears that they are already being discriminated against in their job applications. What greater injustice can afflict a person than to have his application for medical recognition rejected, and yet also to be discriminated against when applying for a job because of some physical or mental handicap? Apart from being deprived of the prospect of earning a living or having a meaningful working life, there is again the possibility of discrimination when it comes to marriage. And this possibility has already materialized, as I understand it. The time has come for the patients and their supporters to be prepared to join and fight to overcome these problems.

There is one final thing I would like to add. Among the films of Tsuchimoto Noriaki is one entitled *The Shiranui Sea*. The opening scene of this film is among the most moving of any film I know. First there appears a caption, "December 1973, Tsukinoura, Minamata Bay." Then we see a lone old man standing on a beach. He picks up an oyster from a rock on the beach and mutters "Oysters are on the increase. Give us another couple of years and there should be quite a lot more of them."

What a poignant comment! The shellfish of Minamata Bay were all killed by poisonous waste water discharged by Chisso. But around 1973, some twenty years later, oysters began to reappear. This is the cause of the old fisherman's rejoicing. It appears the sea is recovering. However, the sea has not really revived. Even today, fish and shellfish caught in the bay cannot be eaten. Nonetheless, the fisherman is happy to see the oysters, signs of life, returning to the bay.

It is this sort of attitude which is so characteristic of the thinking of the antipollution movement. Tsuchimoto might just as easily have started the other way round. He could have made the point that the sea is dead, and since the sea is dead the oysters are inedible. The fact that they are inedible is a reality. But even though the oysters are inedible, the fisherman is delighted. What he longs for and prays for is the revival of the sea. This is the essence of the thinking of the antipollution movement. The reappearance of oysters doubtless pleases the Chisso Corporation, the Kumamoto prefectural government, and the Environmental Agency as well. But is there not a slight difference between the rejoicing of the fisherman-victim on the one hand and that of the Environmental Agency and the Chisso Corporation on the other? In that slight difference it goes without saying that there is actually a vast gulf.

The fight against pollution can be waged by taking up brutal and appalling facts and thrusting them forward as evidence of pollution. This is the way to fight. There is, however, another way, a way of presenting the facts. I believe we are distancing ourselves from the hearts of the fishermen. When we prosecute our claim by triumphantly reciting item by item the damage that has been done, we forget how much the fishermen long for life to return to the sea. It is this sentiment of prayer for regeneration, of longing for resurrection, that must be our starting point for the antipollution movement. On the one hand, there is a fathomless abyss of despair. On the other, there is at the same time prayer and hope for the restoration of nature, and the will and desire to live as human beings. The battle between this despair in life and longing for regeneration is the antipollution movement's battle. If we have only despair, without the desire for regeneration or the resolve to live, the antipollution movement will never become truly a movement of the people.

It is for this reason that I was so moved by the first scenes

of Tsuchimoto's *The Shiranui Sea*, in which the solitary old fisherman rejoices over the return of the oysters. It represents an
unrelenting pursuit of the truth of the harm done, and at the
same time a heartfelt longing for the regeneration of mother
nature and the happiness of the victims as human beings. It
seems to me that, as long as it combines pursuit of the truth
with this natural sensitivity, the antipollution movement will
win a place in the hearts of the people.

I am very fond of the phrase, "God resides in little things."
Kuno Osamu used these words as the title of his book, and they
are beautiful words. The whole resides in the part, the universal in the particular. In the life of a congenital Minamata disease
sufferer is contained the meaning of education, the meaning of
life.

There was an ophthalmologist in Minamata by the name of
Tanigawa who had about him something reminiscent of the
samurai of olden times. One spring day in 1956, Dr. Hosokawa,
head of Chisso Hospital, was playing *gō* with Dr. Tanigawa when
news of the outbreak of a strange disease reached them. His
son, Tanigawa Gan, then a young man in his thirties, was home
at the time recuperating from some ailment. As more and more
reports of cases of the strange disease came in, Gan urged Dr.
Hosokawa to read Henrik Ibsen's play *An Enemy of the People*.
This is a drama about a young man who is driven out of his
village as an enemy of the people for pointing out that the waters
of a newly discovered hot spring, which the villagers were so
pleased to have found, are poisonous. It was a most appropriate
play to recommend.

Three years later, in 1959, young Tanigawa moved to
Nakama in the north of Kyushu and started a magazine called
Circle Village. In the foreword to the first issue were the words,
"It is within the village that the prefecture exists." What did
this mean? The magazine was published as a medium of communication by a group of activists who were dotted about seven
prefectures in Kyushu and Yamaguchi Prefecture in Honshu.

In other words these eight prefectures were in their "Village." And in a symbolic sense, any prefecture is within the village, and Japan itself is within the village.

To know Minamata is to understand Japan. From Minamata, Japan becomes visible. And so I have entitled this chapter "Thoughts from Minamata."

Concluding Remarks

"A blizzard rages, and in the dark of the night a lone traveler spurs on his horse across the snowy plains. He has lost his way and is tired. Seeing a light ahead, he draws close and, as luck would have it, finds an inn. He asks for lodging for the night, and the landlord is astonished. 'Which direction have you come from?' he asks. When the traveler answers, the innkeeper cries out, 'By what stroke of fate have you been spared? So at last the lake has begun to freeze over.' Whereupon the traveler, overwhelmed with horror, suddenly collapses on the floor."

I read this story in a tome of German *gestalt* psychology during my student days.

In the autumn of 1941, I was concentrating on my graduation thesis, graduation that year having been specially brought forward to a date in December. Anyway, I expected that the new year would bring my conscription orders. So I thought I would write what I wanted to write. I wrote a most unsociological dissertation on the subject of "Society and the Individual," and I attached this story as a preface.

Why had the German psychologist introduced this story? It was to explain the notion of object in *gestalt* psychology. The traveler's action is not the crossing of the lake but the galloping over the snowy plains. The psychologist called this action on the snowy plains behavior in the field of action. He called the geographical circumstances of which the traveller was ignorant the local field. The action in the local field could not be called action in the true sense of the word; it was no more than movement. The object in psychology is behavior in the field of action, not movement in the local field.

When I read this explanation I recall wondering what the object of sociology was. Are not what this psychologist termed behavior in the field of action and movement in the local field both objects of sociological study? Sociology must grasp the overall circumstances, taking into its field of vision the traveler, the innkeeper, the blizzard, the snowy plains, and the lake. Indeed I would go so far as to say that the question of the field of study, whether psychology or sociology, is irrelevant. I suppose that at that time I had an interest in how man grasps the wholeness of the world and what sort of relationship he has with the world.

This story also provided me with the opportunity to think about consciousness and action. When I read it, I felt it provided an excellent metaphor for the circumstances of Japan and the Japanese people at the time. Were we not even then galloping across the frozen lake as if it were a snowy plain? It seemed to me that the lake must have an objective existence, even if it did not enter the traveler's field of vision. Man is bound to be led into dangers and catastrophe when there is a wide gap between subjective field of vision and objective existence.

In the thirties, many people enthusiastically studied Marxism. According to Marx, man is free when he recognizes and takes action in the directions dictated by the laws of social development and the inevitability of history. There was a certain persuasiveness in this, even though there was debate over what position should be assigned to spontaneous free will in the zone lying between consciousness and action.

There was, however, something else which drew me to the German story: my interest in existentialism.

Those who believe in the inevitability of history do not give due consideration to the many instances that go together to make up the behavior of the individual within history. The countless deeds of individuals accumulate, and in most such individual deeds there is a social orientation. Consequently the inevitability of history systematically becomes reality.

For example, however fine a man the individual capitalist might be, the social role he performs is seen exclusively as that of a member of the capitalist class. But men who are on their way to the battlefield cannot be so categorized; they are concerned over their own fate as individuals, whether they will be able to remain alive. Without denying the existence of the objective world, at the same time the subjective world too, for the individual, is irreplaceable. It so often happens that young people who are against war end up being killed in battle while soldiers guilty of repeated atrocities survive. How should we react to the irreplaceability of the life of the individual tossed about in the greater currents of history? It is a problem which at one time troubled young men cast into the violent storm of war. It troubled me too.

Let us turn to consider the story of the traveler in the context of the present day. What are we galloping headlong toward now? If we were to encounter some peril now, would it be because of thin ice, physical or mental fatigue, exhaustion on the part of our horse, or hunger? Or is there perhaps no danger? Will the blizzard perhaps cease, a weak sun begin to shine, and the traveler reach the inn unscathed? During the war I believed Japan was galloping over thin ice, but sooner or later I foresaw that defeat would come. I was correct in that prediction. Now, however, I do not have the confidence to look a third of a century ahead. Are there not many others who feel the same way?

One group of Japanese intellectuals in the thirties was confident that it possessed a consciousness of the inevitability of history. It may be going too far to say that the framework of consciousness that sustained that confidence has collapsed, but it certainly has developed cracks. Is it possible, instead, to see ahead into the future of Japan using the framework of the new social sciences? I have my doubts.

Why has such a situation arisen? For one thing, the problems faced by mankind over the past third of a century have been too great for the existing framework of our consciousness. Many social scientists put forward their own strategies for the world, but there is now no precise understanding of the character of the blizzard, the snowy plains, and the lake.

What should the traveler in the blizzard do? Of course the wisest course would be to measure the thickness of ice on the lake before crossing, but he has not the time to wait for proper measurements to be taken. Inevitably, he will find himself making rough measurements in an effort to understand the nature of his surroundings. He will consider how tired he is, and how tired his horse is. All that crosses his mind is the desire to be helped, the expectation of finding some habitation, the will to struggle on, and the boldness to decide on a final plan.

I think the same is true of mankind as a traveler on earth. It is difficult to point to an absolutely safe and wise path, but it is better to have a rough understanding than none at all. It is better to wish to cherish the values of peace, democracy, and human rights than to have no ideas at all. It is better to have the will to protect one's own life and happiness than to lose heart. Come what may, man takes a stand on the subjective world of his experience and begins to act; he does not wait to undertake a thorough investigation of the topography before setting out, nor can he wait. He is being neither nihilistic nor pessimistic nor agnostic. He is following the basic laws of human consciousness and action.

That story aroused my interest in an existentialist way during the war. How would the young of today react? The imagination of young people today would be captured, I believe, by the image of the traveler and the circumstances that surround him. But they would not see that at once. What is urgently needed now is for rough comprehension to be transformed into a more-or-less accurate map. And to effect this transformation what we must do, it seems to me, is to bring together, to create an encounter between, our rough comprehension and our un-embellished hope and determination. In doing so, however, we must not believe we have hit upon absolute answers.

Immediately after the war, it seems to me that to some extent this process of encounter was carried on in a lively fashion; now it is in decline. Is it not of great importance for society that we fuse our powers of comprehension, our sensitivity, and our power to act, and that as a result we strengthen each other? Unless we do so, I fear there is a danger that we may once again fall into the lake.

Memorandum
June/July 1945

Some years ago I came across a copy of a memorandum which I had submitted to the Navy Technical Institute. I have already written (in Chapter Three) my present thoughts about this. It was mere daydreaming, but I hope I will be forgiven for introducing part of it here as a material relevant to understanding the thoughts of one young man on the future of Japan at a time when the end of the war was approaching.

I recall that it was written in June and the first half of July of 1945. Since the original document was quite long I have abbreviated it here.

OPINION CONCERNING A CHANGE OF NATIONAL POLICY

I. Basic Condition of the Great East Asia War and World Trends

Fundamental changes in the domestic political system match sudden new developments in foreign policy; sudden changes in foreign policy likewise call for reform of the domestic political system. The character and purpose of the China affair and the Great East Asia War are such that inevitably the two bear an intimate relationship. This is also in conformity with the general trend of world progress. I wish now to speak frankly about the causes, character, and purpose of the China affair and the Great East Asia War and to point to the inevitability of a change in our national policy. . . . It is my belief that the basic causes of the China affair were: 1. China was seen as the only way to break out of the impasse that our capitalist economy was in. 2. It was hoped that the internal problems and the confused situation that existed from around the time of the 26 February 1936 Incident could be solved by diverting attention to foreign problems. 3. The character of the Chinese people's independence movement was such that it inevitably developed into an antiimperialist movement and came to be led and to be exploited by the Guomindang and the Chinese Communist Party. . . .

Frankly, I take the view that the basic cause of the China affair was that our capitalist economic system needed to seize the China market. The way that, from the time of the Manchurian Incident, the catch phrase ''Protect Our Rights and Interests'' was endlessly repeated must still be fresh in all our memories. To sum it up in a phrase, the China affair was in great part, even if one would not go so far as to say totally, determined by the preoccupation with rights and interests. This is not too different from Anglo-American style imperialism. However, I do not take the view that the China affair was just an aggressive war. It is well known that Japanese capitalism encountered many difficulties and obstacles because it developed later than in Europe and America. And, during this period, our people in all strata of society nursed deep in their hearts the sense that it was Japan's great mission to liberate Asia from European and American control. . . .

Under these circumstances the Great East Asia War broke out. . . . In my private thoughts, I saw the war as bearing a dual character: on the one hand, the fate of our capitalist economy was staked upon it; on the other, it was aimed directly at the liberation of Asia from European and American aggression. If the authorities were to change the character of the Great East Asia War so that it represented only the latter aspiration, a truly earth-shattering change in world history would thereby be accomplished. But unfortunately the authorities lack such discernment, and so the Great East Asia War has reached its present juncture. . . .

Let me make myself quite clear. It is precisely this dual character of the Great East Asia War that is the greatest factor responsible for the plight the country now faces. Our war aims have undergone a great advance, or a great change of character, compared to the time of the Manchurian Incident. The simple preoccupation with rights and interests has been swept aside and we talk instead of "the eight corners of the world under one roof" or the "construction of a new order in East Asia." Why is it, however, that the number of Asian people who follow Japan in its crusade for the liberation of Asia under such slogans, and who pledge solidarity forever, are so few? It is because in terms of fundamental principle our Great East Asia War retains its dual character. In concrete terms, our policy throughout the China affair has been dualistic, and we have given the impression not only to the Chinese people but to the people of Asia that our words are always at odds with our deeds, leading them to think that while we voice fine words what we do is to pursue our self-interest in the most crafty and contemptible way. Since we failed utterly to win the hearts and minds of the Chinese people, other Asian peoples too have shown an uncooperative attitude toward our prosecution of the war. . . .

In what direction are world trends now developing? Politically, toward the freedom and independence of peoples; economically, toward mutual cooperation without exploitation or subordination, both within countries and in relations between them. The two possess a close relationship, and one cannot be realized without the other. People may say that the influence of the middle and small nations seems to be getting ever slighter under the tyranny of the great powers or that the aggressive policies of Anglo-American economic imperialism, though hidden behind fine words about mutual economic cooperation, are actually being pushed to their ultimate. But, as I see it, it seems clear that Britain and the United States are already in deep trouble. The world has been thoroughly awakened to the attempt by the great powers to control it by despotism and dictatorship, despite the self-righteous desires of the United States and Britain. Further, the strategy of capitalist exploitation has reached a real impasse, both at home and abroad, and the realization is gradually growing that such exploitation is in deep contradiction with the principles of democratic freedom which they proclaim. This is especially so in the case of the British Empire. The largely unexpected Labour Party rout of the Conservative Party in the British general elections is actually just a partial expression of this distress. Thinking people can clearly foresee that after the war the United States too will experience acutely this distress which is intrinsic to the capitalist economic system. The problems of freedom, self-government, and the independence of peoples are indeed the greatest problems in Asia.

However, it is a matter for the deepest regret that there are some among our country's wartime leaders and among our people living in the military-occupied areas who do not perceive this worldwide trend but think only of securing economic rights and interests and replacing Europe and America as masters of East Asia. It is the utmost stupidity for the great powers of the world to imagine they can forever carry on the process of scrambling for colonies. Actually, through each such scramble the colonies are gradually being liberated. There are many short-sighted people who say that the reason for the failure of our administration of colonies is that Japan is lacking in experience at controlling other peoples while the British and Americans have long experience. I believe that, however skilled one may be, oppression is oppression and exploitation is exploitation. Of course there are differences. As Gandhi and Nehru put it, it is better for India to be ruled by Britain than to be ruled by Japan. However, they are not saying that for this reason they want to be ruled forever by Britain.

If only Japan would set aside its orientation toward rights and interests and not only aid the self-government and independence of peoples but also understand and give a clear lead in the direction of really progressive social reform by granting freedom of opinion to the various nations and turning an attentive ear to their true voice, then the Great East Asia War would develop in reality as well as in name into an Asian liberation war, and from China through the nations to the south and to the peoples of India it would encourage the trend to participation in the movement for liberation from colonial dependence till it reached cyclone proportions. As a result, difficulties would only spur the people to greater and greater courage so that, despite their material might, the United States and Britain would not be able to withstand the trend. . . .

Let me make so bold as to state my opinion once again. Even if, by some misfortune, the Great East Asia War were to conclude with our defeat, its historical importance for the world would still not be lost. Half of Japan's goals, the most important half, will to some degree have been accomplished. However inept the policies adopted in Japan itself may have been, at least Japan has given independence to oppressed peoples. Burma, the Philippines, Annam, and Cambodia are cases in point. And presently an independent government will be set up in the East Indies. Should the day of Japan's ill fortune dawn, Ba Maw's Burma and Laurel's Philippines might collapse, but it is not difficult to see that Britain, Holland, and France are deeply worried over how to go about reestablishing their control. Their slogan is liberty, and at least they will have to pay more respect than before to the wishes of the people of these regions. They may have no alternative but to grant independence. In that event, the significance of the Great East Asia War will be seen to lie in that it was actually a positive step forward for the peoples of Asia, and at least half the honor for having given the lead will be seen to rest with Japan.

My proposal is this. If the worst comes to the worst and the enemy, the United States and Britain, demands unconditional surrender, we should make a bold response. We should propose a conditional peace. Under what conditions? We demand the independence of Burma. We demand the independence of the Philippines. We demand the independence of the East Indies and the former French colonies. We demand self-government for the Malayan people. We demand the liberation of the Chinese people from semicolonial subordination. We oppose the establishment of British control over Hong Kong (to this end, we should ask the naval authorities to return Hong Kong to the Chinese people without further delay). And Japan should recognize the independence of Korea. Concerning ourselves there is no need to add a single word. Then we should appeal to world opinion. The goal of our Great East Asia War lies in these points. I believe without a shadow of doubt that the goal of the liberation of the peoples of Asia has been accomplished at least to some degree. We can afford to smile at the demise of the Americans and British as they lose power as a result of our demands. We may indeed lose power now, but is it not as clear as day that it is thanks to our power that independence has been granted to the people of Burma and the Philippines and elsewhere? The United States and Britain declare that they will liberate Asia, and, if they fear God, will not dare to take away the rights of independence and self-government from peoples to whom it has once been granted. So our purpose has been accomplished. As for power, I believe in the principle that the will of those without power is also just. . . .

When we search our hearts, we must acknowledge as a fact that in the past we looked upon the granting of national independence as a means to control other peoples, and we should be ashamed of this. So, at this final stage of the Great East Asia War, what I feel bound to call for is that we should make our war aims completely simple and clear. This amounts to a reversal of national policy both at home and abroad. . . . As I have out-

lined above, I believe that the major trends in world affairs
and the character of the Great East Asia War have become
clear. I have therefore set out below my detailed outline for a
fundamental change in our national policy.

II. The Inevitability of a Change in National Policy and an Outline Plan

Before speaking about the inevitability of a change in national policy and outlining a concrete plan, let me first turn my
thoughts back to our national tradition. . . . I am absolutely convinced that to overcome the present national crisis we need
sweeping reform on the scale of the Taika Reform or the Meiji
Restoration. . . .

Next I point to the inevitability of a change in national policy.

1. The basic principle to be observed in effecting a change
in national policy while facing the enemy is to rouse the morale
of the people to the maximum by constructing a pure and
unalloyed domestic order based on the essence of the national
polity, while at the same time accomplishing the ideals and objectives of the Great East Asia War, both domestic and foreign,
through a fundamental change in our foreign policies.

2. As already stated repeatedly above, the ideal of the Great
East Asia War is the liberation of the people of Asia. At the
same time, the liberation of the people of Asia is an indispensable precondition for securing peace for our people for ages
to come. So the most urgent problem in the prosecution of the
war is precisely to restore purity and simplicity to the aims of
the war, where they have become impure and dualistic.

3. The main trend in the world is toward self-government
and the independence of peoples. Of course this is not national
self-determination in the narrow sense that was proclaimed after
the First World War. It is based on the principle of mutual
economic aid between the weak nations, and it also takes ad-
vantage of incorporation as self-governing states within the
big countries. Even in such a case, however, political self-

government, nonexploitative economic equality, and the promotion of indigenous culture are adopted as principles. This of course is the ideal, and various struggles will still be necessary after the war before the peoples of Asia can be completely liberated. Eventually, the contradictions inherent in European and American aggressive imperialism and the awakening of the peoples of Asia will lead to the imperialist aggression of Europe and America being driven from Asia. This is recognized as a major trend in the world. Japan for its part must ensure that it maintains cooperative relations at all times with the peoples of Asia. We must not follow the Europeans and Americans by pursuing self-interest and distancing ourselves from the collective will of the peoples of Asia. That would lead to the worst possible results for Japan. Therefore, the Euro-American capitalist character of our domestic system must be reformed.

4. Particular attention must be paid to trends in neighboring China. We can see that the day is not far off when the forces of Yan'an will rapidly grow and eventually come to control the whole of the country. Among the policies now being proclaimed by Yan'an are some, such as in particular the independence and freedom of peoples and opposition to imperialism, which in their essence are in conformity with our state policies too. In my view, the ultimate basis of our foreign policy should be peace and good relations between China and Japan. I believe particular attention should be paid to this point in revising our national policies.

5. Next, let us consider the economic conditions of postwar Japan. Whether we win or lose the war, our postwar economic recovery will be up against extremely difficult conditions. . . . I will not speak here of the technical conditions needed to overcome these difficulties but will confine myself to outlining only the simplest and most basic principle. That is that the people must bear an equal share of these difficulties. The problem is one of morality and humanity, not just of economy. If on the one hand the privileged are warmly clothed and with full stom-

achs and petty capitalists for whom money is everything proliferate, while on the other the starving collapse on the streets and the numbers of the unemployed mushroom, then there is bound to be a bloody catastrophe. Therefore a change of national policy to eliminate in advance the root of this potential disaster is even more urgently needed than anything to do with specific postwar economic problems.

In addition to the above memorandum, I made various other proposals on both domestic and foreign policy which I will list briefly: reform of the capitalist system so that after the war the peoples of Asia do not again become objects of capitalist exploitation; promotion of enterprise control by groups of workers (unions); state control of enterprises that is not to be equated with supervision by bureaucrats; implementation of an eight-hour working day and a weekly rest system; an end to land-lordism, and promotion of owner-farmer agriculture; state-run health and education; and recognition of freedom of opinion, assembly, and organization. . . .

In terms of foreign policy, policy towards China should be taken as the root of our foreign policy. All economic rights and interests should be returned to the Chinese people, and Taiwan and Hong Kong should be returned. Manchuria should be turned over to self-government by the people of Manchuria. The rights to independence and self-government of the people of Southeast Asia should be recognized. And in Korea, self-government should be implemented in order to promote a Korea for the Koreans. . . .